Essential
Florida

by Emma Stanford

Emma Stanford has written books and
articles on Florida, California, the Caribbean,
Hawaii, France and Spain, as well as
Mediterranean port guides for the US Navy.
She has also contributed to guides published
by the BTA, American Express and Fodor.

Above: *a killer whale in action at Miami Seaquarium*

AA Publishing

Written by Emma Stanford

First published 1998
Reprinted Feb, Apr, Aug and Oct 2000
Reprinted 2001. Information verified and updated.
Reprinted Feb and May 2002

© Automobile Association Developments Ltd 1998
Maps © Automobile Association Developments Ltd 1998

Published by AA Publishing, a trading name of Automobile Association Developments Limited, whose registered office is Millstream, Maidenhead Road, Windsor, Berkshire SL4 5GD.
Registered number 1878835.

Above: *crinolined Southern belles stroll among the floral displays at Cypress Gardens*

A CIP catalogue record for this book is available from the British Library.

ISBN 0 7495 1910 X

Find out more about AA Publishing and the wide range of services the AA provides by visiting our web site at www.theAA.com

Colour separation: Pace Colour, Southampton
Printed and bound in Italy by Printer Trento S.r.l.

Contents

About this Book

KEY TO SYMBOLS

✚ map reference to the maps found in the What to See section

✉ address or location

☎ telephone number

🕐 opening times

🍴 restaurant or café on premises or near by

Ⓜ nearest underground train station

🚌 nearest bus/tram route

🚉 nearest overground train station

✈ travel by air

ℹ tourist information

♿ facilities for visitors with disabilities

✋ admission charge

↔ other places of interest near by

❓ other practical information

▶ indicates the page where you will find a fuller description

---

Essential *Florida* is divided into five sections to cover the most important aspects of your visit to Florida.

Viewing Florida pages 5–14
An introduction to Florida by the author.
Florida's Features
Essence of Florida
The Shaping of Florida
Peace and Quiet
Florida's Famous

Top Ten pages 15–26
The author's choice of the Top Ten places to see in Florida, listed in alphabetical order, each with practical information.

What to See pages 27–90
The four main areas of Florida, each with its own brief introduction and an alphabetical listing of the main attractions.
Practical information
Snippets of 'Did you know...' information
4 suggested walks
4 suggested tours
2 features

Where To... pages 91–116
Detailed listings of the best places to eat, stay, shop, take the children and be entertained.

Practical Matters pages 117–24
A highly visual section containing essential travel information.

Maps
All map references are to the individual maps found in the What to See section of this guide.
For example, Palm Beach has the reference ✚ 29F2 – indicating the page on which the map is located and the grid square in which the resort is to be found. A list of the maps that have been used in this travel guide can be found in the index.

Prices
Where appropriate, an indication of the cost of an establishment is given by **£** signs:
£££ denotes higher prices, **££** denotes average prices, while **£** denotes lower charges.

Star Ratings
Most of the places described in this book have been given a separate rating:
✪✪✪   Do not miss
✪✪   Highly recommended
✪   Worth seeing

Viewing
Florida

Above: one of Miami's art deco hotels
Right: a life-guard on duty

5

Emma Stanford's Florida

Conchs and Crackers
It sounds like a Floridian snack food, but Conchs and Crackers are in fact original Florida residents. As well as being an edible mollusc, a conch (pronounced 'conk') is a Florida Keys resident, born and bred. A Cracker is a descendant of the pioneer farmers, so named for the cracking of their cowmen's whips, or for the cracked corn used to make grits.

Below: smiles speeding by on the sidewalks

Neon nights on Miami Beach's Ocean Drive, oysters in Apalachicola, kayaking on the Blackwater River in the Panhandle and sundowners in Key West are just a few great memories of Florida. It is a popular misconception that Florida's charms are limited to its famous theme parks and its beautiful beaches. While the Sunshine State can certainly lay claim to some of the best of both in the world, there is a great deal more to engage first-time, third-time or even serial visitors.

If you are looking for sophistication, it can be found at a price in a selection of fabulously exclusive hotels and some very good restaurants. Miami, in particular, is a new and shining star in America's culinary firmament. But the real point of Florida is accessibility. Along with sunny skies and affordable prices, the state offers an unrivalled package of family fun and sightseeing opportunities, plus outdoor activities from golfing and watersports to fishing and hiking.

Florida makes an ideal two-centre holiday destination. A week of theme parking in Orlando is just about all the human body can survive – and afford. This is the one time Florida sightseeing gets seriously expensive. Beyond the theme parks there is a terrific choice of beachfront resorts and golf courses, and the contrasting attractions of glitzy Miami, with its Latin American pzazz, and the laid-back Florida Keys. Northern Florida is a well-kept secret, reminiscent of the Old South. Here, intrepid visitors will find a perceptible change of pace, accents like molasses, historical sites and awesome beaches that are rarely visited by international travellers.

Left: shells, found or bought, make popular souvenirs

Florida's Features

Geography

- A low-lying, limestone peninsula bordered by Georgia and Alabama to the north, Florida is the 22nd largest state in the US at 58,625 square miles.
- From the Georgia border, it is just over 420 miles due south to Key West, which is the most southerly point of the continental US, and a mere 90 miles from Cuba.
- The state's 1,790-mile coastline is lapped by the Atlantic Ocean to the east and the Gulf of Mexico to the west. There are 1,094 miles of beaches, and nowhere in the state is more than 60 miles from a beach.
- Average annual temperatures during the summer are 26.9°C in northern Florida and 28.1°C in southern Florida. Average annual winter temperatures are 11.7°C in northern Florida and 20.3°C in southern Florida.
- The highest point in the state is 345ft above sea level.
- The state capital is Tallahassee.

Economy

- Tourism is Florida's number one industry. In 1999, an estimated 58.8 million visitors (7.5 million from overseas) arrived in Florida, generating billions of revenue dollars.
- Agriculture is the second largest earner, chiefly sugar cane around Lake Okeechobee, timber and citrus. Florida supplies over 70 per cent of the US citrus harvest.
- Cattle-ranching and Marion County's thoroughbred horse industry are also major sources of revenue.

People

Florida's population of around 15.1 million is concentrated in the south and coastal cities. The original Cracker farmers are alive and kicking in rural areas, notably in the north. Down south there is a more exotic cultural mix with a large and powerful Cuban community in Miami joined by more recent refugees from Haiti, Nicaragua and other Latin American countries. Florida's Native American population is also based down south. Both the Seminole and smaller Miccosukee tribes operate semi-autonomous reservations in and around the Everglades.

Below: *relaxing on Miami Beach*
Inset: *a resident of Ybor City*

Essence of Florida

One of the crew at the Kennedy Space Center

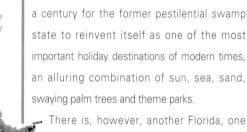

Florida is quite a phenomenon. It took less than a century for the former pestilential swamp state to reinvent itself as one of the most important holiday destinations of modern times, an alluring combination of sun, sea, sand, swaying palm trees and theme parks.

There is, however, another Florida, one blessed with weird and wonderful wildlife and a surprising history preserved in ancient Indian shell mounds, Spanish forts and fancy Victorian historic districts. Step briefly off the beaten track, usually no more than ten minutes off the highway, and here you will find the quirky and intriguing essence of the 'Real Florida'.

THE **10** ESSENTIALS

If you only have a short time to visit Florida, or would like to get a really complete picture of the region, here are the essentials:

• **Get a tan** – but however short your stay, treat the Florida sun with respect. Take it very gently and use a high factor sunscreen, and if you do burn the good news is that soothing aloe vera gel is a local product.

• **Ride a roller-coaster** – you have not done Florida until you have sampled a roller-coaster ride. Some of the best are found at Tampa's Busch Gardens (➤ 64).

• **Visit a state park** – not only a chance to get to grips with the great outdoors, but many of Florida's state parks also protect historical sites.

• **Watch a sunset** – sunset celebrations are big news on the Gulf Coast. Mallory Square in Key West (➤ 18–9) hosts the most famous nightly sunset party.

• **Bring a snorkel** – as well as a live coral reef off the Florida Keys, there are

numerous dive sites around the state.

• **Take a boat trip** – nature trips, canoe adventures, fishing expeditions and sunset sails; it is easy to take to the water in Florida.

• **Collect shells** – beaches on the Gulf of Mexico are the best for shell collecting, particularly the islands of Sanibel and Captiva (➤ 24).

• **Meet a manatee** – either in the wild or at rescue and rehabilitation units within aquariums, such as SeaWorld (➤ 60) and the Miami Seaquarium (➤ 36).

• **Travel into space** – it is not yet possible to sign up for a Shuttle trip, but the next best thing is to watch a launch from the Kennedy Space Center (➤ 17).

• **Take mosquito repellent** – absolutely essential when visiting parks and reserves. Mosquitoes love nice humid, jungly swamps and woodland areas.

Above: *top up your tan on Cocoa Beach*

Above: *a quiet moment of evening sun over Panama City Beach, the Panhandle's busiest resort*

Facing page: *a boat tour of the Everglades*

9

The Shaping of Florida

c10000 BC
Groups of primitive hunter-gatherers arrive in the Florida peninsula, concentrating in the coastal regions.

c5000 BC
Semi-permanent village settlements appear along the St Johns River.

AD c1000
Evidence of agriculture and increasingly sophisticated religious and cultural practices.

1513
Spanish explorer Juan Ponce de León lands near the site of present-day St Augustine in April, and names the New World territory La Florida.

1521
De León returns with 200 settlers, but the colonists are driven out by warring Calusa Indians. De León dies of an arrow wound in Cuba.

Hernando de Soto, governor of Florida, attacks native chiefs

1539–59
Spanish attempts to settle in the Tampa and Pensacola regions fail.

1564–5
French Huguenots establish Fort Caroline on the St Johns River, but are massacred by the Spanish. Pedro Menéndez de Avilés founds St Augustine, the oldest continuously inhabited European settlement in the US.

1600s–1700s
Pirates and privateers harry Spanish treasure fleets returning from South America along the Gulf Stream. Colonisation continues slowly into the northern Panhandle.

1763–83
The British occupy Florida for 20 years before the colony is returned to Spain under the Second Treaty of Paris.

1776
The American Declaration of Independence.

1817–18
Friction between white settlers and Florida's Native American Seminole population results in the First Seminole War.

1821
Spain cedes Florida to the United States in settlement of a debt of $5 million.

1824
The Indian village of Talasi is selected as the site of the proposed state capital and renamed Tallahassee.

1835–42
Second Seminole War. In 1842, the US Army escorts 3,000 Seminoles along the Trail of Tears to face exile on reservations to the west of the Mississippi.

1845
Florida becomes the 27th state of the Union.

1861–5
Florida is one of the first states to secede from the Union and join the Confederacy at the start of the Civil War.

10

1868
A new constitution extends the vote to all male citizens over 21, including blacks.

1870s
Steamboats plying the St Johns River ferry Florida's first tourists.

1886
Henry Flagler begins construction of the Florida East Coast Railroad and a chain of luxurious beach hotels along the Atlantic Coast. Henry Plant builds a cross-state railroad to Tampa on the Gulf Coast.

1894–5
The Great Freeze decimates Central Florida's citrus groves.

1902
The first automobile races are held on Daytona Beach.

1914
The world's first scheduled air service is inaugurated, flying between St Petersburg and Tampa.

1920s
Vast fortunes are made and lost in the Florida Land Boom.

1947
President Truman is present at the opening of the Everglades National Park.

1958
NASA (National Aeronautics and Space Administration) selects Cape Canaveral Air Force Station as a test ground for early rocket and satellite programmes.

1965
Walt Disney announces his intention to create a theme park in the vicinity of Orlando.

1969
Apollo 11 blasts off from the Kennedy Space Center for the first moonwalk mission.

1971
Magic Kingdom opens, the first phase of Walt Disney World.

1980
Over 125,000 Cuban refugees land in Florida in the Mariel boatlift.

1992
Hurricane Andrew hits South Florida causing $25 billion worth of damage and 15 deaths.

2000
The presidential election is decided in Florida. George W Bush eventually wins after recounts delay the result for several weeks.

The US Astronaut Hall of Fame, on the Space Coast

Peace & Quiet

Above: *a lizard basks in the midday sunshine in the Marie Selby Gardens, Sarasota*
Opposite: *nearly 100 black bears are killed every year on Florida's roads*

Just a step away from teeming theme parks, space-age technology and burgeoning urban centres, Florida can boast more than 50 state parks, swathes of unspoilt forest and undeveloped beaches, and 10 national parks. Visitors in search of peace and quiet need look no further.

Wildlife Habitats

Poised on the boundary that divides the temperate north from the sub-tropical south, Florida showcases an extraordinary diversity of natural habitats and wildlife. The Everglades National Park (➤ 41) alone harbours more than 2,000 plant species flourishing in the immense sawgrass wetlands, punctuated by hardwood hammocks, pockets of oak, mahogany, gumbo limbo and other native trees that have found purchase on rock outcrops above the swamp. These hammocks are a refuge for animals such as racoons, deer and bobcats, and birds. The best time to visit the Everglades is during the winter dry season when the waters recede and wildlife is concentrated around ponds and gator holes, pools dug out by American alligators in their search for a cool place to lie in the heat of the day.

Wet woodland areas make for excellent birdwatching.

One of the finest spots is the National Audubon Society's Corkscrew Swamp Sanctuary (► 41), with a winding boardwalk trail through cypress woods and a good chance of spotting eagles, buzzards, woodpeckers, herons and storks.

Coastal mangrove belts are a favourite breeding and feeding ground for water birds, sea turtles, fish, alligators and a few rare American crocodiles. Manatees are also found here, though the gentle giant sea cows are equally at home in freshwater rivers further inland, and the warm springs where they prefer to congregate in winter. Some of the best places to see manatees are Blue Spring State Park (► 53) and Homosassa (► 54) in central Florida.

Rare Species

A few remaining Florida panthers stalk the Everglades, but are unlikely to survive the on-going destruction of their once-extensive hunting grounds. Rare black bears are occasionally seen in the pine woodlands of central Florida's Ocala National Forest (► 59), though wild turkeys and armadillos snuffling about in the undergrowth are a more common sight. Also on the endangered list are the tiny Key deer found on Big Pine Key in the Florida Keys (► 47). The smallest sub-species of the Virginia white-tailed deer, these dainty creatures grow to just 24–28 inches high.

A heron at rest in the Everglades

From May to September, sea turtles come ashore to lay their eggs on Florida's sandy beaches. Loggerheads, leatherbacks, and green turtles dig nests in the sand and each lay around 100 eggs which hatch after approximately 60 days. The nesting grounds are protected by law, and bright lights are forbidden as they may confuse the hatchlings who are guided to the sea by moonlight.

Outdoor Activities

Florida's numerous parks offer a wide range of outdoor activities. As well as short nature trails and longer hiking paths, there may be cycle paths, ranger-led walks, fishing and boating, and scuba-diving in freshwater springs. Canoe trails are also popular at riverfront parks.

BEAR CROSSING

Florida's Famous

The celebrated author Ernest Hemingway penned several of his novels at his Key West home

Literary lions
The lion that roars the loudest in Florida's literary pantheon is probably Ernest Hemingway, who wrote several of his finest works while living in Key West. Also in the 1930s, Marjorie Kinnan Rawlings won a Pulitzer prize for *The Yearling*, her account of Florida backcountry life, and Zora Neale Hurston wrote in the language of the rural black south. Notable modern Florida writers include Connie May Fowler and satirical thriller writer Carl Hiaasen.

Henry Morrison Flagler

Born in Hopewell, New York, Henry Flagler (1830–1913) was already a rich and successful businessman when he first visited Florida in the early 1880s. Flagler fell in love with the winter climate and determined to create a 'Southern Newport', where the wealthy and fashionable could disport themselves during the long northern winters. His magnificent Ponce de Leon Hotel (now Flagler College) in St Augustine (► 22) opened in 1888, the first of a chain of luxurious resorts linked by his own East Coast Railroad. The chief architect of Florida's early tourist industry, Flagler set up home in Palm Beach (► 21), and his famous 'Railroad to the Sea' finally reached Key West in 1912.

Marjorie Stoneman Douglas

Writer, feminist and Florida's most famous environmentalist, Marjorie Stoneman Douglas (1890–1998) arrived in Miami in 1915. Working for her father, editor of the *Miami Herald*, Douglas graduated from society editor to columnist and began to publish the vivid Florida short stories with which she first made her name. In 1947, her classic portrait of the Everglades, *The Everglades: River of Grass* was published in the year President Truman dedicated the Everglades National Park. Twenty years later, aged 78, she became a voluble and effective eco-warrior, founding the conservationist group Friends of the Everglades to challenge developers and fight for government legislation to protect the fragile Everglades ecosystem.

Christine Marie (née Evert) Lloyd

Chris Evert bestrode the courts of the international tennis circuit throughout the 1970s and early 1980s. Born in Fort Lauderdale in 1954, she was taught initially by her tennis coach father and played in her first tournament at the age of eight. In a professional career lasting from 1971 to 1989, she chalked up 18 grand slam singles titles, at least one every year between 1974 and 1986. Nicknamed the 'Ice Maiden', Evert was renowned for her powerful ground stokes and double-fisted backhand which revitalised the modern women's game.

Top Ten

Above: *a queen angel fish*
Above right: *Palm Beach County's colourful emblem*

1
Art Deco District, Miami

 32C2

Cafés/restaurants
(£–£££)

C, H, K

Art Deco Weekend, Jan

Art Deco Welcome Center

 1001 Ocean Drive

305/672 2014

Mon–Fri 11–6, Sat
10–10, Sun 11–10

Self-guided audio tours
available daily 11–4.
Walking tours, Thu
6.30PM and Sat
10:30AM. Cycle tours on
the third Sun of the
month at 10:30AM from
Miami Beach Bicycle
Center, 601 5th Street,
reservations 305/
674 0150

*Eye-catching art deco
architecture on Miami's
Ocean Drive*

*Brilliant, funky and fun, Miami Beach's
celebrated Art Deco District is a slice of history and
one of the hippest spots on the planet.*

Hot movie location and fashion shoot backdrop of the
1990s, chic playground of the glitterati from Gloria Estefan
to Madonna, the Art Deco District has come a long way
from the dingy, run-down neighbourhood the City of Miami
was anxious to bulldoze in the 1970s. Even with a listing
on the US National Register of Historic Places, the first
20th-century site to be recognised, the battle is not over
for the 800-plus significant buildings in an area running
north from 6th Street to 23rd Street, and east–west from
Ocean Drive to Lenox Avenue.

Ocean Drive is the epicentre of the neighbourhood. This
strip of glamorous oceanfront hotels showcases three basic
architectural styles: the traditional art deco buildings of the
early 1930s; the rounded corners, racy lines and aero-
dynamic styling of Streamline Moderne; and a selection of
classical Mediterranean Revival edifices. A special feature
of Miami's art deco style is the frequent use of tropical
motifs such as palm trees, exuberant foliage and graceful
flamingos. The strikingly bright pastel colour schemes are a
modern departure designed to highlight these entertaining
decorative devices. The **Art Deco Welcome Center**
provides maps and details of guided tours. A night-time visit
is highly recommended for the amazing neon.

2
Kennedy Space Center

*Mission control for the American space programme
opens its doors to the public with a flourish of
space hardware, IMAX films and tours.*

One of the state's top visitor attractions, the Kennedy
Space Center offers an unrivalled opportunity to get behind
the scenes of the space race, take a look at its history,
marvel at the technology and catch a glimpse of what may
be in store for astronauts in the 21st century.

NASA (National Aeronautics and Space Administration)
first set up a Florida facility in 1958, at the nearby Cape
Canaveral Air Force Station. This original base for the early
Mercury and Gemini programmes and its museum is one
of the bus tours available. The first launch from the
Kennedy Space Center was *Apollo 8* in 1968. A year later
Apollo 11 put Neil Armstrong on the moon. Today, there
are regular Space Shuttle launches from Launch Complex
39, which is on the not-to-be-missed Kennedy Space
Center bus tour. This tour also includes close up views of
the landmark VAB (Vehicle Assembly Building), the
giant crawler-transporters which trundle the
Shuttles to the launch pad at a sedate
1mph, the International Space Station and
the excellent Apollo/Saturn V Center which
contains a complete 363ft Saturn V rocket
in the main hall and a launch presentation
in the Firing Room Theater.

The Visitor Complex contains a
number of diversions including
the Galaxy Center where the
big-screen IMAX cinemas
are located. Exhibits
include displays of
space vehicles, and
artefacts from moon
dust and model Lunar
Rovers to space suits.
There are presentations
in the Universe Theater
and the child-friendly
Robot Scouts show,
and don't miss out on
a stroll around the
towering exhibits in
the   Rocket
Garden, then stop
by the Astronaut
Memorial.

✚	29E4
✉	SR405, Merritt Island (off US1 N of Cocoa)
☎	321/452 2121 or 1-800 572 4636
🕐	Daily 9–dusk
🍴	Mila's Roadhouse Grill (£–££), cafés and snack concessions (£)
♿	Very good
✋	Very expensive; includes exhibits, bus tour and IMAX show
?	KSC bus tours run throughout the day; check schedules for Cape Canaveral tours. Space Shuttle launch info ☎ 321/867 4636

*Make friends
with an
astronaut at
the Kennedy
Space
Center*

3
Key West

Original furnishings at Ernest Hemingway's house in Key West

America's southernmost city, Key West lies at the end of the Florida Keys, torn between an agreeable tropical stupor and the demands of tourism.

 29E1

 Cafés/restaurants (£–£££)

402 Wall Street/Mallory Square ☎ 305/294 2587

Conch Republic Celebration, Apr–May; Hemingway Days, Jul

Aubudon House

 205 Whitehead Street

☎ 305/294 2116

🕐 Daily 9:30–5

✋ Moderate

Hemingway House

✉ 907 Whitehead Street

☎ 305/294 1136

🕐 Daily 9–5

♿ Good

✋ Moderate

Venture on to bustling Duval Street, Key West's touristy main thoroughfare, or attend the famous nightly sunset celebrations on Mallory Square pier, and the instant impression is of an island city under siege. But step away from the crowds and the quirky capital of the Conch Republic retains a unique charm in its local character and leafy lanes.

In its early days, Key West was a pirates' lair, later settled by wreckers. These 19th-century salvage operators amassed considerable fortunes and built some of the city's finest architecture, including Key West's Oldest House, which is now a rather ramshackle museum. Other fine examples of historic Key West homes are the lovely **Audubon House**, visited by famous naturalist and painter John James Audubon in 1832, and the **Hemingway House**, where Ernest Hemingway lived and worked in the 1930s.

The most famous Key West wrecker of modern times is Mel Fisher, who spent 15 years locating

and salvaging the Spanish galleons *Atocha* and *Santa Maria*, lost off the Keys in 1622. Gold jewellery and other artefacts from the $400 million treasure trove are on display in the fascinating **Mel Fisher Maritime Heritage Society Museum**. Near by, the Key West Aquarium reveals underwater mysteries of a different order, including brilliantly coloured tropical fish, sharks and sea turtles.

For the best view of Key West, climb the 110ft Key West Lighthouse. The huge lens is still in working order, and there is a museum laid out in the former keeper's quarters. Another worthwhile stop is the East Martello Museum, which combines local history exhibits with an art gallery.

Key West Lighthouse was built in 1848

Mel Fisher Maritime Heritage Society Museum

✉ 200 Greene Street

☎ 305/294 2633

🕐 Daily 9:30–5

♿ Good

✋ Moderate

Mallory Square is an ideal place to buy souvenirs and to stop for a coffee

4
National Museum of Aviation

This state-of-the-art aviation museum combines Top Gun fun with a fascinating insight into the history of flight.

 28A5

 1750 Radford Drive, Pensacola Naval Air Station

 850/453 2389

 Daily 9–5

Café (£)

Very good

Free. Charge for IMAX cinema and flight simulator

 Pensacola (▶ 86)

 Guided tours on request

Above: sleek blue Skyhawks are a major attraction at the National Museum of Aviation

Over 170 aircraft, airships and space capsules have been packed into the cavernous halls of this huge museum, laid out in the historic Pensacola Naval Air Station. There is a glass atrium big enough to hold four A-4 Skyhawk jets, once flown by the US air force's Blue Angels display team and now suspended from the roof in flying formation, a full-size re-creation of a World War II aircraft carrier flight deck, complete with a line-up of fighter planes, and numerous 'hands-on' simulators and interactive displays.

The guided tours are a highlight of the museum. Although all the exhibits are accompanied by storyboards, the tours, led by volunteers who are often veteran pilots, add an unbeatable insider view. They can also point out some of the more esoteric exhibits it would be easy to miss, such as trainee World War II pilot George Bush's logbook, a little slice of history from long before he rose to become America's President and Commander-in-Chief.

Several of the museum's larger exhibits are parked out on the runway and open to inspection. There are also tours of Fort Barrancas, overlooking Pensacola Bay. Spanish colonists first occupied the site in 1698, and it attracted the attentions of the US Army during the 1840s. The fort's Advance Redoubt is an open site a short drive away.

5
Palm Beach

A fortuitous shipwreck sowed the seeds for Palm Beach, and railway baron Henry Flagler provided that little extra something – money.

In 1878, a cargo of 20,000 coconuts washed up on Palm Beach and obligingly sprouted into an idyllic tropical backdrop for one of Henry Flagler's splendid resorts. Architect Addison Mizner was equally charmed by his surroundings in the 1920s, and launched a welter of Mediterranean Revival designs that helped shape the style of Florida's most exclusive seaside community. Today, Palm Beach is a millionaire's playground of luxurious mansions, manicured lawns and black-belt shopping, where the smell of money is palpable. For around nine months of the year things are relatively quiet, but Palm Beach's winter social season is in a class of its own as old money, new money, players and playboys descend for an orgy of parties, polo and charity balls.

Despite the exaggerated country club atmosphere, tourists are welcome. The 4½-mile Palm Beach Bicycle Trail covers the local highlights, including the **Flagler Museum** in Whitehall, Henry Flagler's sumptuous Palm Beach residence. There are tours of the lavishly furnished 73-room mansion crammed with French, Italian and English antiques, and the private railway carriage in the grounds is a miniature work of art. A hidden treat along the route are the lovely Cluett Memorial Gardens behind the Episcopal Church of Bethesda-by-the-Sea.

The twin poles of Palm Beach's social whirl are the glorious Breakers Hotel and the elegant shopping enclave of Worth Avenue, nicknamed 'Fifth Avenue South' for its dazzling collection of designer boutiques and up-market jewellery stores (► 104). Tucked away behind the main thoroughfare is a maze of delightful little Addison Mizner-designed courtyards containing smaller shops, galleries and cafés.

✚	29F2
🍴	Cafés/restaurants (£–£££)
ℹ	45 Coconut Row
↔	West Palm Beach (► 49)

Flagler Museum

✉	1 Whitehall Way
☎	561/655 2833
🕐	Tue–Sat 10–5, Sun 12–5. Closed Mon
♿	Good
✋	Moderate

Breakers, the grandest hotel in Palm Beach

6
St Augustine

29E5

Cafés/restaurants
(£–£££)

10 Castillo Drive
☎ 904/825 1000

Arts and Crafts Festival,
Mar; Founding
Anniversary, Sep

Castillo de San Marcos

1 Castillo Drive

☎ 904/829 6506

Daily 8:45–4:45
(restoration will limit
access during 2001–2)

Limited

Moderate

Regular tours

*The Oldest House, on St
Francis Street, dates
from the early 1600s*

*The oldest continuously inhabited European
settlement in the US, St Augustine predates the
arrival of the Pilgrim Fathers by half a century.*

Though several attempts were made to establish a
foothold in Florida earlier in the 16th century, St Augustine
was founded in 1565 by Pedro Menéndez de Avilés, the
newly-appointed Spanish governor of Florida dispatched by
Philip II of Spain to rout the fledgling French colony at Fort
Caroline (➤ 81).

St Augustine is a delight and small enough to explore on
foot, though there are mini sightseeing trains and horse
and carriage rides from Avenida Menendez, north of the
Bridge of Lions. The original settlement was razed to the
ground by Sir Francis Drake in 1586, but it was rebuilt in
the shadow of the **Castillo de San Marcos**, an imposing
star-shaped fortress built of limestone from Anastasia
Island across the bay. The Spanish garrison lived with their
families in the town and one of their homes, the Oldest
House, has been restored. Each room is furnished to
depict a different period in its remarkable history.

Henry Flagler honeymooned in St Augustine in 1883,
heralding St Augustine's Gilded Age. One of Flagler's
former hotels, the Alcazar, now houses the Lightner
Museum with its fabulous collections of fine and
decorative arts dating from this period. Since then the city
has added all manner of museums and historic 'experiences' – see the St Augustine walk (➤ 87).

7
St Petersburg

A trio of world-class art museums have transformed sunny St Petersburg into a leading cultural hot spot.

Once regarded as the Gulf Coast's chief roost for elderly 'snowbirds', or winter visitors, St Petersburg has spruced up its image considerably in recent years. St Pete (as it is familiarly known) is the cultural centre of the Pinellas Suncoast resort area (➤ 63) a half-hour drive away.

The grid of broad and tree-shaded downtown streets leads down to Tampa Bay and a causeway anchoring The Pier shopping, dining and entertainment complex to the mainland. Just to the north of here is the **Museum of Fine Arts** housed in an attractive Mediterranean style villa. The collections start with ancient Greek and Roman sculpture, then move through the major periods of European art to 19th- and 20th-century American works. Asian, African, pre-Columbian and Native American arts and crafts are also well represented.

Also on the waterfront, the **Salvador Dali Museum** boasts the largest collection of the surrealist artist's work outside Spain. The guided tours are excellent, and the imaginative gift shop does the artist proud.

The **Florida International Museum** is a vast exhibition space which hosts major touring exhibitions every year – past crowd-pullers have included Treasures of the Tsars from the Kremlin Museum and Alexander the Great, in conjunction with the Greek Ministry of Culture.

✚ 29D3

Museum of Fine Arts

✉ 255 Beach Drive

☎ 727/896 2667

🕐 Tue–Sat 10–5, Sun 1–5

✋ Moderate

Salvador Dali Museum

✉ 1000 3rd Street S

☎ 727/823 3767

🕐 Mon–Sat 9:30–5:30, Sun 12–5:30

✋ Moderate

Florida International Museum

✉ 100 2nd Street N

☎ 727/822 3693

✋ Expensive

The Pier's profile makes a distinctive landmark

8
Sanibel & Captiva Islands

Shell collecting is an absorbing pastime on Bowmans Beach

A brace of lovely barrier islands linked to the mainland by a causeway, Sanibel and Captiva are havens for shell collectors and beach lovers.

29D2

1159 Causeway Boulevard, Sanibel
941/472 1080

Sanibel Shell Fair, Mar

Bailey-Matthews Shell Museum

3075 Sanibel-Captiva Road, Sanibel

941/395 2233

Tue–Sun 10–4

Good

Cheap

J N 'Ding' Darling National Wildlife Refuge

Sanibel-Captiva Road

941/472 1100

Refuge: Sat–Thu 7:30AM to sunset; Visitor Center: Sat–Thu 9–5 (May–Oct 9–4)

Good

Refuge: Cheap. Visitor Center: free

According to local legend, 18th-century pirate José Gaspar once stowed his female captives on these lush islands, famous for their pristine, soft sandy beaches and relaxing atmosphere. Holidaymakers looking for an action-packed time should avoid Sanibel and Captiva, though there are plenty of sightseeing opportunities across the causeway in Fort Myers (➤ 44–5). Apart from lazing in the sun, the few island sights are low key. But there are activities, including fishing, golfing, and exploring the cycle paths, and boat trips from local marinas, where it is also possible to rent sailboats and canoes.

The famous beaches are on the Gulf side and they are liberally sprinkled with a fantastic variety of seashells, from the common whelk to speckled junonias and more exotic finds. The best time to look is at low tide or after a storm, but be warned: live shelling is illegal and punishable by jail and a fine. Amateur shell collectors and full-blown conchologists alike should take the time to stop off and inspect the **Bailey-Matthews Shell Museum**, which fields exhibits on shell lore and arts as well as collections of shells from around the world.

The other 'must-see' attraction on the islands is the **J N 'Ding' Darling National Wildlife Refuge**, a 5,600-acre wetlands preserve with a 5-mile self-guided wildlife drive (there are narrated tram tours in winter), walking paths and canoe trails. Resident wildlife to look out for includes alligators, osprey, roseate spoonbills and hawks. The drive is best at low tide first thing in the morning or in the evening when the wading birds are feeding (tickets are valid all day).

9

Sarasota

Sarasota's lively cultural scene owes much to circus impresario John Ringling, who created a waterfront estate to house his art collections.

Copies of classical statues overlook visitors to the Ringling Museum

An appealing, small-scale waterfront city combining a handful of diverse sight-seeing attractions, easy access to the Tampa Bay area, superb barrier island beaches, and an enviable calendar of performing arts events, Sarasota makes an excellent holiday base.

The city's crown jewel is the **Ringling Estate**, a 38-acre bayfront spread incorporating John Ringling's magnificent 1920s Venetian-style winter residence Ca'd'Zan ('House of John' in Venetian dialect), a museum of baroque and Renaissance art, and a circus museum full of colourful and curious Big Top memorabilia. The jewel-like 18th-century, 300-seat Asolo Theater may also be open to view.

Down by the waterfront, the gorgeous Marie Selby Gardens are a botanical feast for the eye, planted with a colourful array of hibiscus, cacti, bromeliads and bamboos. The orchid collection is famous and there is an interesting tropical foods section, as well as a butterfly garden and exhibitions of botanical illustrations.

John Ringling employed circus elephants to help build the causeway across to St Armand's Key, and designed St Armand's Circle, Sarasota's most exclusive shopping enclave. To the south, Lido Key is a popular resort area offering family beaches and watersports. There are public access footpaths to the hotel-lined sands of Longboat Key, and a popular attraction in this neck of the woods is the Mote Marine Aquarium. A research and educational facility, the Mote's centrepiece is a huge shark tank. Other diversions include rescued sea turtles and manatees and touch tanks stocked with crabs and rays. The pelican sanctuary across the car park is also well worth a visit.

29D3

655 N Tamiami Trail
☎ 941/955 0991 or
1-800 800 3906

Sarasota Jazz Festival, Mar; Music Festival, Jun

Ringling Estate

✉ 5401 Bayshore Road/US41

☎ 941/359 5700

🕐 Daily 10–5:30

✋ Moderate

10
Walt Disney World® Resort: Magic Kingdom Park®

The biggest thing to hit Florida tourism since the railroad, Walt Disney World continues to set the standard for theme parks worldwide.

60A2

Lake Buena Vista (20 miles south of Orlando)

Information, 407/824 4321; reservations, 407/934 7639

Check current schedules

Each park offers a good choice. Make bookings at Guest Relations for table service restaurants (££–£££)

Free shuttle bus from many Orlando/Kissimmee hotels

Excellent

Very expensive (➤ 71, panel)

Daily parades, shows and night-time fireworks and laser displays

Animator and entrepreneur Walt Disney opened his first theme park in California in 1955. Disneyland was an immediate success, but Disney loathed the commercial sprawl that sprang up around the site and resolved to control every aspect of his next venture. In the early 1960s, he secretly amassed a vast land holding outside Orlando, and the Magic Kingdom, the first phase of the resort, opened in 1971, to be followed by Epcot, Disney-MGM Studios and the latest blockbuster, Disney's Animal Kingdom, which opened in spring 1998 (➤ 70–1).

Based on the original Disneyland prototype, the Magic Kingdom is Disney's most popular Florida park and should not be missed. Its seven themed lands radiate from the fairytale Cinderella Castle, each providing an imaginative selection of rides and shows. In Adventureland, for instance, there are rip-roaring adventures with the Pirates of the Caribbean and a steamy Jungle Cruise. The Big Thunder Mountain roller-coaster and Splash Mountain flume ride are highlights of Wild West-themed Frontierland. Riverboat rides depart from the Liberty Square colonial quarter, which is also home to the entertaining Haunted Mansion and educational Hall of the Presidents, which delivers a potted history of the USA through the mouths of former presidents. Mickey's Toontown Fair and Fantasyland are the little children's favourite lands, hosting a galaxy of best-loved cartoon characters and specially scaled down rides. In Tomorrowland old favourites such as the excellent and popular Space Mountain roller-coaster have been joined by the creepy thrills of the ExtraTERRORestrial Alien Encounter and Buzz Lightyear's Space Ranger Spin featuring a laser shoot-out against the evil Zurg.

Cinderella Castle

What to See

Above: *a Bengal tiger at Miami's Metrozoo*
Right: *the funnel of the riverboat* Jungle Queen

27

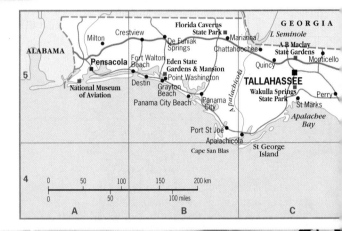

ALABAMA

Milton Crestview

Pensacola Fort Walton
Beach

National Museum
of Aviation

Destin

De Funiak
Springs

Florida Caverns
State Park ● Marianna

Chattahoochee ●

Eden State
Gardens & Mansion
● Point Washington

Grayton
Beach
Panama City Beach ● Panama
City

Quincy

TALLAHASSEE

GEORGIA
L Seminole

A B Maclay
State Gardens

● Monticello

Apalachicola

Wakulla Springs
State Park

● Perry

● St Marks

*Apalachee
Bay*

Port St Joe ●

Apalachicola

Cape San Blas

St George
Island

0   50   100   150   200 km

0   50   100 miles

A   B   C

4

5

Did you know ?

*A delightful spot to take a break on any tour of
Coral Gables is the Venetian Pool. Fed by a natural
spring, the miniature blue lagoon was carved out of
an old stone quarry and landscaped with a sandy
beach and Venetian-inspired bridges and changing
room buildings. The pool is closed on Mondays.*

FLORIDA

St Marys

Fernandina Beach
Amelia Island
White Springs
Osceola National Forest
JACKSONVILLE
Mayport
Live Oak
Lake City
Orange Park
Jacksonville Beach
Branford Starke
St Augustine
Gainesville
Chiefland
Micanopy
Palatka
L.
■ Alligator Farm
■ Marineland of Florida
uwannee
Manatee Springs State Park
Silver Springs
George
Ormond Beach
Daytona Beach
edar Key
Ocala
Ocala National Forest
Blue Spring State Park
Leesburg
Mount Dora
Homosassa Springs State Wildlife Park
Brooksville
Sanford
Orlando
Titusville
Weeki Wachee
Walt Disney World Resort
Universal Studios
Kennedy Space Center (NASA)
Dade City
Rockledge
Cape Canaveral
Tarpon Springs
Fantasy of Flight
Sea World
Kissimmee
Cocoa Beach
Dunedin
Lakeland
Winter Haven
Lake
FLORIDA'S TURNPIKE
Melbourne
Clearwater
Largo
✈**TAMPA**
Bartow
Kissimmee
Vero Beach
St Petersburg
Cypress Gardens
Lake Wales
Bok Tower Gardens
Tampa Bay
Gamble Plantation
Sebring
Intracoastal Waterway
Fort Pierce
Ringling Estate
Bradenton
Bellm's Cars & Music of Yesterday
Arcadia
Lake Placid
Okeechobee
Stuart
Sarasota
Peace
Venice
Port Charlotte
Lake Okeechobee
Jupiter
Punta Gorda
Riviera Beach
Juno Beach
■ Marinelife Center
Captiva
Caloosahatchee
Clewiston
West Palm Beach
■ Palm Beach
Cape Coral
Fort Myers
Belle Glade
Boynton Beach
Sanibel
Edison Home
Corkscrew Swamp Sanctuary
Delray Beach
Caribbean Gardens
The
Boca Raton
Naples
Everglades
Fort Lauderdale
Pompano Beach
ALLIGATOR ALLEY
Plantation
Big Cypress National Preserve
Hollywood
Everglades City
North Miami Beach
Gulf
Hialeah
Miami Beach
of
✈**MIAMI**
Mexico
Metrozoo
Biscayne National Park
Everglades National Park
Monkey Jungle
Cape Sable
Mangrove Swamp
Florida City
Flamingo
Key Largo
Florida Bay
Islamorada
Fort Jefferson
Big Pine Key
Straits of Florida
Dry Tortugas
Bahia Honda State Park
Marathon
Florida Keys
Key West

D   E   F

St John's River

Suwannee

DeLand

Miami

Big, brash and sexy, Miami comes on like a Hollywood starlet displaying her attractions in an enviable tropical setting. The palm trees, the shimmering beaches, the wide blue skies and the sailboats skimming across glittering Biscayne Bay are just as they should be. The vertiginous downtown skyline serves the joint purpose of sightseeing attraction and a measure of the city's recent success. This is a city on the make and it does not care who knows.

Miami has an intriguingly international flavour. Poised at the gateway to Latin America, there is a touch of salsa in its soul and a large and voluble Cuban community who know how to make good coffee and dine late. Europeans have also made inroads, particularly in SoBe (South Beach), the terminally hip Miami Beach Art Deco District, whose unique brand of cutting edge kitsch has become an international style icon.

> '*Miami's neon glitter and pulse of Broadway are tempered by the languor of the tropics, and time is as negligible as yesterday's weather report.*'
>
> The WPA Guide
> To Florida (1939)

Miami

It is little more than a century since pioneer Julia Tuttle lured Henry Flagler and his railroad south with a bouquet of orange blossom despatched during the devastating 1894–5 Great Freeze in central Florida. Today, the sprawling bayfront metropolis has a population of 2 million and ranks as the third most popular city destination in the US after Los Angeles and New York.

Bathed in neon, the impressive NationsBank building towers over downtown Miami

The main resort areas are on Miami Beach, with the Art Deco District in the south, the major hotels in the middle, and more budget-orientated options in the north. On the mainland, downtown is well supplied with executive-style hotels, there are a few upmarket choices in Coconut Grove and Coral Lakes, or smart resorts on Key Biscayne, and budget places near the airport. Miami's sights are widespread, with several family-orientated attractions a good 45-minute drive south of downtown. To get the most from a stay of more than a couple of days, a car is helpful.

What to See in Miami

ART DECO DISTRICT (► 16, TOP TEN; ► 34, WALK)

BASS MUSEUM OF ART

Tucked away in a small grassy park, the Bass is a real treat laid out over two floors of a 1930 art deco building. European old master paintings, drawings and sculpture from the Renaissance, baroque and rococo periods are augmented by a superb collection of 16th-century Flemish tapestries. There are more modern works and collections of antique furniture and *objets d'art*. Special exhibits focus on the many different strengths of the permanent collections, and the museum hosts a broad-ranging programme of visiting exhibitions and weekend cultural events.

✚ 32C3
✉ 2121 Park Avenue, Miami Beach
☎ 305/673 7530
🕐 Tue, Wed, Fri 10–5, Thu 1–9, Sun 1–5
🚌 G, K, L, S
♿ Good
🍽 Moderate

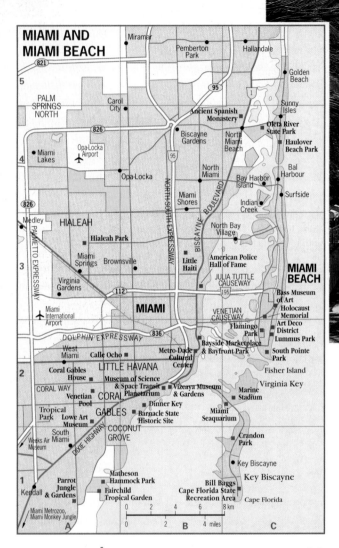

MIAMI AND MIAMI BEACH

Miramar • Pemberton Park • Hallandale
821
5 • Golden Beach
PALM SPRINGS NORTH • Carol City 95 1 • Sunny Isles
Ancient Spanish Monastery • Oleta River State Park
826 • Biscayne Gardens North Miami Beach • Haulover Beach Park
• Miami Lakes Opa-Locka Airport 95 North Miami • Bal Harbour
Opa-Locka • Bay Harbor Island • Surfside
Miami Shores • Indian Creek
826 • Medley North Bay Village
HIALEAH • North Bay Village
Hialeah Park Little Haiti • American Police Hall of Fame
Miami Springs Brownsville JULIA TUTTLE CAUSEWAY
4 MIAMI BEACH
Virginia Gardens 112 • Bass Museum of Art
Miami International Airport VENETIAN CAUSEWAY • Holocaust Memorial
MIAMI 836 Flamingo Park • Art Deco District
DOLPHIN EXPRESSWAY Bayside Marketplace & Bayfront Park Lummus Park
West Miami • Calle Ocho Metro-Dade Cultural Center • South Pointe Park
Coral Gables House LITTLE HAVANA Fisher Island
CORAL WAY Museum of Science & Space Transit Planetarium Vizcaya Museum & Gardens Virginia Key
Venetian Pool CORAL GABLES • Dinner Key Marine Stadium
Tropical Park Lowe Art Museum Barnacle State Historic Site Miami Seaquarium
South Miami COCONUT GROVE
Weeks Air Museum DIXIE HIGHWAY Crandon Park
Matheson Hammock Park • Key Biscayne Key Biscayne
Parrot Jungle & Gardens Fairchild Tropical Garden Bill Baggs Cape Florida State Recreation Area Cape Florida
Kendall
Miami Metrozoo, Miami Monkey Jungle

0   2   4   6   8 km
0   2   4 miles

A   B   C

✝ 32B2

✉ 401 N Biscayne Boulevard

☎ 305/577 3344

🕐 Mon–Thu 10–10, Fri–Sat 10–11, Sun 11–9

🚇 College/Bayside

🚌 C, S, 16, 48, 95

BAYSIDE MARKETPLACE ✪✪

A waterfront shopping, dining and entertainment complex, downtown Bayside is a popular stop on the tourist trail. The open-air mall features around 150 boutiques and gift stores, a Hard Rock Café, a food court, cafés, bars and restaurants. Free entertainment is provided by wandering street performers and there is live music nightly. Bayside is conveniently accessible by water taxi, and regular Biscayne Bay sightseeing cruises depart from the dock.

COCONUT GROVE ✪✪✪

The Grove is one of Miami's oldest and most appealing neighbourhoods. Once a byword for Bohemian living, recently the neighbourhood has been shaken from its reverie by an influx of bright young things, and the busy junction of Grand Avenue and Main Highway has been inundated with smart little shops and galleries, pavement cafés and the CocoWalk shopping centre. However, the atmosphere is still relaxed and friendly and it is a great place to hang out. There are historic homes in the pioneer **Barnacle State Historic Site**, hidden in a hardwood hammock on the water, and palatial Vizcaya (► 37). The 1920s Coconut Grove Playhouse is also worth visiting for its elaborate Spanish-style stucco façade and reputation as a leading local repertory theatre.

CORAL GABLES ✪✪

A gracious product of the 1920s land boom, the leafy residential enclave of Coral Gables is deemed grand enough to have its own driving tour. Maps are available from the City Hall, on Miracle Mile, and stops along the way include the fabulous Biltmore Hotel (► 100) and developer George Merrick's bijou 'Villages'. These little groups of homes were built in a variety of eye-catching architectural styles, from Chinese to Dutch Colonial.

➕ 32A1
🍴 Cafés/restaurants (£–£££)
🚌 42, 48
❓ Goombay Festival, Jun

Barnacle State Historic Site
✉ 3485 Main Highway
☎ 305/448 9445
🕐 Fri–Sun, tours at 10, 11:30, 1, 2:30
♿ Limited
💲 Cheap

➕ 32A2
🍴 Cafés/restaurants (£–£££)
🚌 24, 72

Above: *lively Miamarina in Bayside Marketplace*

33

A Walk Around South Beach

Distance
Just over 2½ miles to Bass
Museum; 4-mile circuit to
Welcome Center

Time
2 hours with coffee stops and
browsing. Add at least an hour
for a visit to the museum

Start/end point
Ocean Drive
✚ 32C2
🚌 C, H, K

Lunch
Wolfie's (£)
✉ 2038 Collins Avenue
☎ 305/538 6626

*The haunting Holocaust
Memorial is set around a
tranquil lily pond*

This walk starts at the Art Deco Welcome Center (► 16),
and heads north on Ocean Drive to 15th Street, past a
showcase array of delectable deco delights.

*Turn left on 15th, left on Collins Avenue,
doubling back for 200yds to a right turn on to
Espanola Way.*

A pretty little Mediterranean pastiche, between Drexel and
Washington Avenues, Espanola is a good place to stop for
coffee and window shopping.

*Continue westwards on Espanola Way to
Pennsylvania Avenue. Turn right and head
north to Lincoln Road; turn left.*

Dozens of galleries, boutiques and café-restaurants have
gravitated to the pedestrian-zoned Lincoln Road Mall. Art
deco highlights include the restored Lincoln Theatre and
the Sterling Building with its glass-block
headband (spectacular at night).

*Head north on Meridian Avenue for
three-and-a-half blocks to the Holocaust
Memorial.*

The centrepiece of this enormously moving
memorial is a giant bronze arm reaching
skyward from a seething mass of doomed
humanity. Victims' names are inscribed on a
memorial wall and the horror of the Holocaust
is described in words and pictures.

*Double back to 19th Street and turn
left alongside the Convention Center
car park. At the top of the street turn
left and look for the canal-side footpath
on the right, which rejoins Washington
Avenue. Cross Washington on to 21st
Street. After a block-and-a-half, the Bass
Museum (► 31) will be found on the
left. Turn right along Collins Avenue,
by Wolfie's famous deli restaurant, and
head south, back towards Ocean Drive,
passing on the way a selection of
Miami Beach's finest hotels.*

FAIRCHILD TROPICAL GARDEN ✪✪✪

These magnificent botanical gardens, the largest in the US, consist of an 83-acre tract of lawns and lakes, hardwood hammocks and miniature rainforest. The palm collection is one of the largest in the world, and there are tropical blooms and a specialist Rare Plant House. A narrated tram tour sets the scene; then you are on your own to explore the trails through coastal mangrove and Everglades areas.

Adjacent to the Fairchild, Matheson Hammock Park is a good place to have a swim and enjoy a picnic.

- ✚ 32A1
- ✉ 10901 Old Cutler Road, Coral Gables
- ☎ 305/667 1651
- 🕐 Daily 9:30–4:30
- 🍴 Café (£)
- 🚌 65
- ♿ Very good
- ✋ Moderate

KEY BISCAYNE ✪✪

Reached by the Rickenbacker Causeway (toll), which affords a fantastic view of downtown Miami, Key Biscayne presents a choice of good beaches. The broad, 5-mile stretch of public beach at Crandon Park is understandably popular, but the **Bill Baggs Cape Florida State Recreation Area** has considerably more to offer for a day out. The 500-acre park was badly hit by Hurricane Andrew in 1992, but the cycling and walking trails, boardwalks and barbecue grills have all been restored or replaced. Fishing is another popular pastime, and the 1845 Cape Florida lighthouse is also open to the public.

- ✚ 32C1

Bill Baggs Cape Florida State Recreation Area
- ✉ 1200 S Crandon Boulevard
- ☎ 305/361 5811
- 🕐 Daily 8AM–sunset
- 🍴 Snack concessions (£)
- ♿ Good
- ✋ Cheap

MIAMI BEACH ✪✪✪

Miami Beach's golden shores are divided up into a number of sections each patronised by a different clientele. The southern reaches around South Pointe Park are popular with surfers and Cuban families. The SoBe (South Beach) section between 5th and 21st Streets is the most hip and crowded, with a gay focus around 12th Street. North of 21st Street, the crowd is more family-orientated, though nude bathing is legal in the northern section of Haulover Park.

- ✚ 32C3
- ✉ Ocean Drive and cross-streets off Collins Avenue. Boardwalk from 21st Street to 46th Street
- 🚌 FM, H, L, S

Miami's art deco hotels make a pleasing backdrop to the busy beaches

MIAMI METROZOO

This huge and attractively laid out zoo features more than 800 animals from 190 species, most of them housed in spacious natural habitat enclosures. The monorail is a good way to get an overview of what is on offer; then be sure to stop off at the Bengal tigers, the koalas, the cute Himalayan black bears and pygmy hippos, and the gorillas. There are wildlife shows throughout the day, and PAWS, the excellent petting zoo area, has elephant rides.

+ 29F1
✉ 12400 SW 152nd Street, South Miami
☎ 305/251 0400
◷ Daily 9:30–5:30

MIAMI SEAQUARIUM

Performances by Lolita the killer whale, Flipper the dolphin, and Salty the sea lion are among the highlights at this venerable sealife attraction. In between the shows and the popular Shark Channel presentations, there are dozens of aquarium displays to inspect, petting experiences and the gently educational manatee exhibit. The Seaquarium is a leading marine research centre and operates a Marine Mammal Rescue Team which cares for injured manatees. These huge but gentle creatures that live in shallow waters are often the victims of boat propellers.

+ 32C2
✉ 4400 Rickenbacker Causeway, Virginia Key (Key Biscayne)
☎ 305/361 5705
◷ Daily 9:30–6
🍴 Various concessions and cafés (£–££)
🚌 B
& Very good
💷 Expensive

MONKEY JUNGLE ✪

Monkey Jungle's special appeal is the free-roaming macaque monkey colony released by Joe Dumond in 1933. Instead of locking up the monkeys at his behavioural research facility turned sightseeing attraction, Dumond decided to cage the visitors by enclosing boardwalk trails through the woodlands. While the descendants of the original six monkeys now scamper about at liberty, most of the other inhabitants, from gibbons and colobus monkeys to tiny tamarins, are securely caged. Monkey programmes and feeding times are scheduled throughout the day.

+ 29F1
✉ 14805 SW 216th Street, South Miami
☎ 305/235 1611
◷ Daily 9:30–5
🍴 Snack bar (£)
& Very good
💷 Expensive

Above: *the immensely powerful Bengal tiger*

MUSEUM OF SCIENCE AND SPACE TRANSIT PLANETARIUM ✪✪✪

A first-class science museum with a raft of imaginative interactive exhibits, this is the place to sample virtual reality basketball, climb a rock wall or enjoy the travelling Smithsonian Exhibitions programme. The natural world is represented in the coral reef and Everglades displays and there is a Wildlife Center where rescued birds and reptiles are rehabilitated for release back into their natural habitats. Regular astronomical presentations take place in the Space Transit Planetarium.

+ 32B2
✉ 3280 S Miami Avenue, Coconut Grove
☎ 305/646 4200
◷ Daily 10–5
🍴 Café (£)
🚇 Metrorail Vizcaya
🚌 48
& Very good
💷 Moderate

PARROT JUNGLE AND GARDENS ✪✪

A major part of Parrot Jungle's attraction are the lush tropical gardens laid out in a comfortably shady hardwood hammock. The parrots are scheduled to move to Watson Island, off Miami Beach, in 2003, so they will be easier to visit and the gardens will be re-created. The troupe of pink flamingos that once starred in the opening credits of the television series *Miami Vice* will survive and there will be parrot shows, a serpentarium, primate area, baby bird nursery and children's petting zoo.

🟫 32A1
✉ 11000 SW 57 Avenue, South Miami
☎ 305/666 7834
🕐 Daily 9:30–6
🍴 Parrot Café (£)
♿ Very good
🎫 Moderate

VIZCAYA MUSEUM AND GARDENS ✪✪✪

Millionaire industrialist James Deering had this splendid Italian Renaissance-style villa constructed as a winter residence in 1914–16. Together with his architect, F Burrell Hoffman Jnr, and designer, Paul Chalfin, Deering trawled Europe for the 15th- to 19th-century antiques that furnish the Renaissance dining room, the rococo salon, and the English-style Adams Library. The formal gardens that lead down to Biscayne Bay are peopled by a wealth of statuary and enclosed by native hardwood trees, while the dock is styled after a Venetian water landing and is protected by a stone gondola.

🟫 32B2
✉ 3251 S Miami Avenue, Coconut Grove
☎ 305/250 9133
🕐 Daily 9:30–5
🍴 Vizcaya Café (£–££)
Ⓜ Metrorail Vizcaya
🚌 48
♿ Reasonable
🎫 Moderate

Vizcaya mansion sits amid striking formal gardens

Southern Florida & the Florida Keys

Less than a century ago, southern Florida was pioneer territory dominated by the mysterious, waterlogged expanses of the Everglades. It is hard to believe today, for this is Florida's most populous and most visited tourist heartland.

Bordering the beleaguered Everglades, the Gold Coast unfurls seamlessly north from Miami to West Palm Beach, combining the accessible attractions of Fort Lauderdale with more exclusive haunts such as Boca Raton and Palm Beach. The southern Gulf coast is only slightly less developed between the twin poles of upscale Naples and Fort Myers. The latter, with a wide range of sightseeing possibilities and the lovely barrier islands of Sanibel and Captiva (➤ 24), makes an especially good family holiday destination.

Trailing off towards the tropics, the Florida Keys provide a somewhat different brand of hospitality and a relaxed style that captures the hearts of many visitors.

> *'Florida…does beguile and gratify me – giving me my first and last (evidently) sense of the tropics…'*
>
> HENRY JAMES
> *Letter to Edmund Gosse*
> (1905)

———————•———————

The Overseas Highway links the Florida Keys

Mizner Park, an impressive shopping mall in Boca Raton

29F1
9700 SW 328th Street, Homestead
305/230 1100
Daily 8–5:30; Visitor Center daily 8:30–5
Good
Cheap

29F2
Boca Festival Days, Aug

International Museum of Cartoon Art
201 Mizner Park
561/391 2200
Tue–Sat 10–6, Sun 12–6
Very good
Moderate

Boca Raton Museum of Art
501 Mizner Park
561/392 2500
Tue, Thu, Sat 10–5, Wed, Fri 10–9, Sun 12–5
Very good
Cheap

What to See in Southern Florida and the Florida Keys

BISCAYNE NATIONAL PARK ⭐

A 181,500-acre park with a surprising difference, namely that over 96 per cent of this national preserve is under water. It protects a live coral reef, which is home to more than 200 varieties of tropical fish, and an 18-mile-long chain of unspoilt island keys notable for marine and bird life. Snorkel and dive trips can be arranged from the Visitor Center at Convoy Point and glass-bottomed boat tours offer an alternative window on the underwater world.

BOCA RATON ⭐⭐

The well-heeled Gold Coast city of Boca Raton is a vision of strawberry ice-cream pink mansions and malls inspired by its Roaring Twenties founder Addison Mizner (► 21), who planned to make it the 'greatest resort in the world'. The land boom crash of 1926 put paid to his grandiose scheme, but several Mizner creations survive, including the exclusive Boca Raton Resort and Club.

Boca has the aura of a giant country club offering golf, tennis, watersports and some lovely beach parks. The two most exclusive (and pink) shopping malls are the Royal Palm Plaza and Mizner Park, which is also home to the **International Museum of Cartoon Art**. The museum is a treasure trove of antique and modern cartoons, comic strip heroes and film shows. Art lovers also have a treat in store at the **Boca Raton Museum of Art**, which features frequently changing exhibitions and the Mayers Collection of works by 19th- and 20th-century artists including Degas, Picasso and Matisse, as well as a sculpture garden.

CAPTIVA ISLAND (➤ 24, TOP TEN)

CORKSCREW SWAMP SANCTUARY ✪✪✪

The National Audubon Society first posted guards on Corkscrew Swamp in 1912 to protect herons and egrets from plume hunters. The 11,000-acre sanctuary is now renowned for its superb bird life (➤ 13) and the nation's largest stand of giant bald cypress trees. An excellent 2¼-mile boardwalk trail traverses the shadowy swamp woodlands, where ancient cypress trees tower up to 130ft high. Some of these rare survivors of the 1940s and 50s Everglades logging booms are over 500 years old. Look for wading birds feeding on the floating lettuce lakes and there may be a glimpse of an alligator or otters.

EVERGLADES NATIONAL PARK ✪✪

The base of the Florida peninsula is like a giant sieve slowly draining the Everglades into the Gulf of Mexico through the maze of the Ten Thousand Islands. The 'river of grass' begins its journey to the sea at Lake Okeechobee and flows southwest into the 1½ million-acre national park, which is a mere fifth of the Everglades' actual size.

There are three entrances to the park, with the main visitor centre on the eastern side, 10 miles west of Florida City. Here, a variety of short boardwalk trails venture into the sea of sawgrass dotted with island hammocks, which offer the best chance of spotting the local flora and fauna (➤ 12–13), there are ranger-led walks and boat rentals at the Flamingo Marina. Tram tours depart from the northern Shark Valley entrance (➤ 108), on US41, 35 miles west of Miami. Canoe rentals and tours are available from the western Gulf Coast Visitor Center, near Everglades City.

Above: *the anhinga, denizen of the Everglades*

🔲 29E2
✉ CR846 (20 miles E of Bonita Springs/US41)
☎ 941/348 9151
🕐 Daily Dec–Apr 7–5; May–Nov 8–5
♿ Good
👣 Moderate

Above left: *the raised boardwalk trail at Corkscrew Swamp Sanctuary*

🔲 29E1
✉ Main Visitor Center, SR9336 (W of US1)
☎ 305/242 7700
🕐 Daily 8–5
🍴 Flamingo (£–££)
♿ Reasonable
👣 Cheap (tickets valid for 7 days)

Gulf Coast Visitor Center
✉ CR29, Everglades City
☎ 941/695 3311
🕐 Daily 7:30–5 in winter, reduced in summer

The Gold Coast

A leisurely day trip with time for sightseeing, this drive follows the Gold Coast north between Fort Lauderdale and Palm Beach.

Begin at the junction of Sunrise Boulevard and South Ocean Boulevard (A1A), and head north on A1A for 14 miles to the junction with Camino Real in Boca Raton. Turn left, passing the Boca Raton Resort and Country Club, then turn right on Federal Highway. Cross Palmetto Park Road and turn right into Mizner Park.

Window shopping at Mizner Park is a favourite pastime in ostentatious Boca Raton (► 40).

Return to Palmetto Park Road. For the direct route to Palm Beach, turn left and rejoin A1A. For an interesting detour, turn right. At Powerline Road (4¹/₂ miles), turn right and head north for 5¹/₄ miles to the entrance to the Morikami Museum and Japanese Gardens.

Chic boutiques are a feature of pink-hued Mizner Park

Distance
50 miles

Time
2 hours. A day trip with stops

Start point
Fort Lauderdale
✚ 29F2

End point
Palm Beach
✚ 29F2

Lunch
Coral Lynn Café (£)
✉ Via de Lela, 240 Worth Avenue, Palm Beach
☎ 561/651 7888

Set in peaceful formal gardens, Japanese cultural exhibits and artefacts are displayed in the Yamoto-kan villa and museum galleries.

Turn left out of the Morikami. At the junction with Atlantic Avenue/SR806, turn right and continue through Deerfield Beach. Rejoin A1A north for 15 miles to a T-junction outside Palm Beach. Bear right for A1A N on South Ocean Boulevard. Just under a mile later, keep right on Ocean Boulevard for just over a mile, then turn left on to Worth Avenue.

Worth Avenue is the gold-plated heart of downtown Palm Beach (► 21).

For a fast return to Fort Lauderdale, take Royal Palm Way (five blocks north of Worth) across to West Palm Beach and follow signs for I-95.

FORT LAUDERDALE

The largest city on the Gold Coast, Fort Lauderdale combines with ease its dual roles of thriving business and cultural centre and popular beach resort. The namesake fort was founded on the New River in 1838, during the Second Seminole War, and the small settlement developed into a busy trading post before the arrival of the railroad. A special feature of the downtown district is the 'Venice of America', a network of canals and islands dredged in the 1920s, which boasts some of the city's most desirable waterfront properties; these are best viewed from one of the regular sightseeing cruises.

The New River meanders through the city centre conveniently linking a handful of historic sites and modern cultural landmarks with the 1½-mile Riverwalk. This landscaped route along the north bank begins at the turn-of-the-century **Stranahan House**, the oldest surviving house in town. The pioneering Stranahans used to entertain railway baron Henry Flagler in their heart pine parlour, and the interior faithfully re-creates a Florida home of 1913–15. There is a small local history museum laid out in a former inn in the Old Fort Lauderdale district, and the Riverwalk ends at the Broward Center for the Performing Arts.

Fort Lauderdale's main shopping and dining district is Las Olas Boulevard, an attractive, tree-shaded street that leads to the **Museum of Art**. The striking museum building is a fitting showcase for extensive collections of 19th- and 20th-century European and American art and visiting exhibitions. Near by, the **Museum of Discovery and Science** is one of Florida's finest, with a spectacular range of exhibits, interactive displays and an IMAX cinema.

29F2
Butterfly World (➤ 108)
Fort Lauderdale Boat Show, Oct

Stranahan House
335 E Las Olas Boulevard (at SE 6th Avenue)
954/524 4736
Wed–Sat 10–4, Sun 1–4
Limited
Cheap

Museum of Art
1 E Las Olas Boulevard
954/525 5500
Tue–Sat 10–5, Sun 12–5
Very good
Moderate

Museum of Discovery and Science
401 SW 2nd Street
954/467 6637
Mon–Sat 10–5, Sun 12–6
Subway Café (£)
Very good
Moderate

Stranahan House was, in its time, considered to be the height of luxury

Bonnet House
- ✉ 900 N Birch Road
- ☎ 954/563 5393
- 🕐 Guided tours Wed–Fri 10–1:30, Sat–Sun noon–2:30
- 💰 Moderate

Above: the Jungle Queen offers day and evening cruises on New River

🔗 29E2
↔ Sanibel and Captiva Islands

Edison Winter Home and Ford Winter Home
- ✉ 2350 McGregor Boulevard
- ☎ 941/334 3614
- 🕐 Mon–Sat 9–4, Sun 12–4
- ♿ Good
- 💰 Moderate

Hidden from view by hardwood hammock behind Fort Lauderdale's sandy beach, the **Bonnet House** is a delightful Old Florida relic. The two-storey plantation-style house was built by artist Frederic Bartlett in 1920 and the interior is a wonderfully eccentric work of art covered in murals, canvasses and decorations fashioned out of beach-combing treasures. In the gardens, black and white Australian swans paddle about a miniature lake flanked by the yellow bonnet lilies after which the house is named.

South along the oceanfront, the 'Yachting Capital of the World' has its HQ at the Bahia Mar marina, where the *Jungle Queen* riverboat departs for New River cruises. Ocean-going voyages set out from Port Everglades, the second largest cruise ship terminal in the world.

FORT MYERS ✪✪

Thomas Alva Edison put Fort Myers on the map back in the 1880s, when the great inventor built himself a winter home in town and planted the first stretch of palms along McGregor Boulevard. Fort Myers now likes to call itself the 'City of Palms' and makes a pleasantly relaxed holiday centre with a family-orientated beach annexe and a good selection of sightseeing attractions in and around town.

The **Edison Winter Home** and adjacent **Ford Winter Home**, built by Edison's motoring magnate friend Henry Ford, are the most visited sights on the local tourist trail. Visits to the Edison home include a tour of the laboratory, which is packed with examples of the great man's inventions, from the phonograph to miner's lamps. Take time to explore the gardens too, which are planted with a great variety of rare and exotic plants that were collected by Edison while wearing his expert horticulturist hat.

Junior scientists will have a field day at the colourful and entertaining **Imaginarium Hands On Museum and Aquarium** with its impressive store of interactive games and gadgets, saltwater and freshwater aquariums, and a cinema presenting 3-D film shows. At the **Calusa Nature Center and Planetarium** getting to grips with Florida's native flora and fauna is the name of the game. In addition to snake and alligator presentations, there are bugs, lizards and touch exhibits, plus nature trails and the Audubon Aviary, a rescue and rehabilitation unit for injured birds.

A short drive east of town, **Manatee Park** is a non-captive haven for manatees. In winter, the observation deck affords a prime view of West Indian manatees basking in the warm run-off waters from a nearby power plant. For animal-spotting with a bit more bite, make tracks for **Babcock Wilderness Adventures** and a bumpy swamp buggy ride around the vast Crescent B Ranch – the tour guides are trained naturalists. As well as bison, quarter horses and Senepol cattle, the ranch is inhabited by wild alligators, hogs, deer and turkeys. The buggies also venture into 10,000-acre Telegraph Swamp, where a boardwalk trail leads to a panther enclosure.

Imaginarium Hands On Museum and Aquarium

- ⊠ 2000 Cranford Avenue
- ☎ 941/337 3332
- 🕐 Tue–Sat 10–5
- 🍴 Imagateria Café (£)
- ♿ Very good
- 💰 Moderate

Calusa Nature Center and Planetarium
- ⊠ 3450 Ortiz Avenue
- ☎ 941/275 3435
- 🕐 Mon–Sat 9–5, Sun 11–5
- ♿ Limited
- 💰 Cheap

Manatee Park

- ⊠ SR80 (1.5 miles E of I-75/Exit 25)
- ☎ 941/432 2004
- 🕐 Daily 8–5 (summer 8–8)
- ♿ Good
- 💰 Free (nominal parking fee)

Babcock Wilderness Adventures

- ⊠ SR31 (9½ miles N of SR78), Punto Gorda
- ☎ 1-800 500 5583
- 🕐 Daily, Nov–Apr 9–3; May–Oct mornings only
- 💰 Expensive
- ❓ Reservations essential

Comfortable wicker armchairs furnish Thomas Edison's home in Fort Myers

ISLAMORADA ✪

The self-styled 'Sport Fishing Capital of the World', Islamorada consists of a clutch of small islands with a concentration of marinas and Florida's second oldest marine park. Charter boats offer half- and full-day expeditions to the rich Gulf Stream fishing grounds. Local dive operators also do good business and there are trips to the uninhabited island preserves of Indian and Lignumvitae Keys from Lower Matecumbe Key.

Sea lion and dolphin shows are on the bill at the **Theater of the Sea**. This old-style attraction includes all the usual shark encounters and touch tanks, and has added a Dolphin Adventure programme which allows visitors to swim with captive dolphins. Understandably popular, the dolphin swim requires reservations (➤ 112).

KEY LARGO ✪✪

Key Largo ('long island' to the early Spanish explorers) is the largest of the Florida Keys, and a lively resort within easy striking distance of Miami. The island makes a great base for divers, who can explore the depths of the magnificent **John Pennekamp Coral Reef State Park**, which extends for over 3 miles out to sea across the living coral reef. Snorkelling and dive trips, equipment and canoe rental, and a dive school are all available, and there are also a range of glass-bottomed boat trips, aquariums in the visitor centre and walking trails on the land-based portion of the park.

Local birdlife is showcased at the **Florida Keys Wild Bird Center** on the neighbouring island of Tavernier. This

---

➕ 29F1

🍴 Cafés/restaurants (£–££)

❓ Sport fishing tournaments throughout the year. For information
☎ 305/872 2233

Theater of the Sea

✉ Mile Marker 84.5
☎ 305/664 2431
🕐 Daily 9:30–4
♿ Good
💰 Expensive

➕ 29F1

🍴 Cafés/restaurants (£–£££)

❓ Island Jubilee, Nov

John Pennekamp Coral Reef State Park

✉ Mile Marker 102.5
☎ 305/451 1202
🕐 Daily 8–5
♿ Good
💰 Cheap

Florida Keys Wild Bird Center

✉ Mile Marker 93.6
☎ 305/852 4486
🕐 Daily dawn–dusk
♿ Fair
💰 Donation

The dazzling white sands of Bahia Honda State Park are backed by dense tropical forest

rescue and rehabilitation facility has a boardwalk trail past enclosures for hawks, ospreys, cormorants and pelicans. There are also birdwatching hides, overlooking a salt pond where herons and roseate spoonbills come to feed.

KEY WEST (► 18–19, TOP TEN)

LOWER KEYS ⭐⭐

South of the minor miracle of the Seven Mile Bridge (in reality 110yds short of seven miles), the Lower Keys are less developed than their northern counterparts. Just across the bridge, **Bahia Honda State Park** is one of the finest natural beaches in the Keys and a regular contender in any list of the nation's top ten beaches. Watersports concessions rent out equipment and snorkels, and behind the white sand shore there are walking trails through tropical forest, where several rare trees and plants can be seen.

The other top attraction in this area is the **National Key Deer Refuge**, centred on Big Pine Key. The deer here are pint-sized relatives of the Virginia white-tailed deer and are best spotted in the early morning and evening. Key Deer Boulevard (Mile Marker 30.5) leads to Blue Hole, a freshwater lagoon in an old limestone quarry. Wading birds gather here to feed, and alligators and turtles occasionally put in an appearance. A little further down the road, Watson's Nature Trail leads off into the forested heart of the refuge.

➕ 29E1

Bahia Honda State Park
✉ Mile Marker 37
☎ 305/872 2353
🕐 Daily 8–sunset
♿ Good
✋ Cheap

National Key Deer Refuge
✉ Refuge Headquarters, Big Pine Shopping Plaza, Big Pine Key (Mile Marker 30)
☎ 305/872 2239
🕐 Refuge, open site; Headquarters, Mon–Fri 8–5
✋ Free

Did you know ?

Dolphin encounter programmes are a special feature of the Florida Keys, offering visitors a chance to swim with these highly intelligent and friendly mammals. Several dolphin research centres and the Theater of the Sea offer dolphin encounters (► 112). Reservations (up to two months ahead) are essential.

📍 29E1
🍴 Cafés/restaurants (£–£££)

Pigeon Key
✉ Visitor Center at Mile
Marker 48
☎ 305/289 0025
🕐 Daily 9–5
♿ Good
💲 Moderate

📍 29E2
🍴 Cafés/restaurants (£–£££)
↔ Corkscrew Swamp
(➤ 41)

Caribbean Gardens
✉ 1590 Goodlette Road
☎ 941/262 5409
🕐 Daily 9:30–5:30
♿ Good
💲 Expensive

Facing page: *Norton
Museum of Art attracts
renowned touring
exhibitions*
Below: *a Yellow Cab in
the chic Old Naples
shopping district*

MARATHON ✪

Strung out in a muddle of malls, motels and small businesses along US1 north of the Seven Mile Bridge, Marathon is the chief town of the Middle Keys, and a rival for Islamorada's sport fishing crown (➤ 46).

Another good reason to visit Marathon is the Museum of Natural History of the Florida Keys (➤ 108). Also, the Old Seven Mile Bridge (which doubles as the World's Longest Fishing Pier) gives access to **Pigeon Key**, a former construction workers' camp from the Flagler era recently restored as a National Historic District.

NAPLES ✪✪

A relaxing, small resort city on the Gulf of Mexico, Naples has beautiful beaches, an attractively restored historic shopping and restaurant district in Third Street South, a thriving Center for the Arts and more than 50 championship golf courses.

Naples lies close enough to the Everglades to make a day trip to the national park's western entrance near Everglades City (➤ 41). Closer to home, visitors to the Naples Nature Center can take to the water on a narrated boat ride, sample woodland nature trails and drop in at the Wildlife Rehabilitation Center, which tends over 1,600 native bird and animal casualties a year.

There are rather more exotic beasts in store at **Caribbean Gardens**, a popular zoological park with a special interest in big cats. Daily shows put a selection of lions, tigers, leopards and cougars through their paces. Many of the animals are the result of the park's successful captive breeding programmes.

PALM BEACH (▶ 21, TOP TEN; ▶ 42, DRIVE)

SANIBEL ISLAND (▶ 24, TOP TEN)

WEST PALM BEACH

The high-rise downtown heart of West Palm Beach faces monied and manicured Palm Beach across the Intracoastal Waterway. While the super-rich cavort in the oceanfront resort, West Palm Beach takes care of business and provides a selection of shopping, cultural attractions and sightseeing opportunities.

The city's pride and joy is the **Norton Museum of Art,** one of the most important art museums in the southeastern US. Built around the collections of steel magnate Ralph Norton (1875–1953), the museum is particularly strong on French Impressionist and Post-Impressionist works (Monet, Matisse, Renoir, Gauguin, Chagall) and 20th-century American art (Hopper, O'Keefe, Pollock), and has a stunning collection of Chinese ceramics, bronzes and jade carvings.

There are several good outings for children. For 'hands-on' interactive fun, the South Florida Science Museum is a big hit. Sparky electricity displays, booming sound waves and a mini tornado are among the treats on offer. Hands-off is the best way to approach the **Lion Country Safari,** a two-part wildlife park that provides some very close encounters with lions, elephants, rhino and giraffes in the 500-acre drive-through African safari section. In the adjacent Safari World Park there are more animals, fairground rides, lagoon cruises and a nature trail.

➕ 29F2
↔ Dreher Park Zoo (▶ 108)
❓ SunFest, Apr–May; Japanese Bon Festival, Aug

Norton Museum of Art
✉ 1451 S Olive Avenue
☎ 561/832 5196
🕐 Tue–Sat 10–5, Sun 1–5
♿ Very good
🎫 Donation

Lion Country Safari
✉ W Southern Boulevard/ SR80 (17 miles W of I-95)
☎ 561/793 1084
🕐 Daily 9:30–5:30
♿ Good
🎫 Expensive

Did you know ?

During the December to April winter social season, polo is a popular Gold Coast sporting fixture. The sport draws a host of celebrity fans from Hollywood stars to royalty, and anyone can rub shoulders with them for the inexpensive price of a ticket (▶ 113).

49

Central Florida

Central Florida's very first theme park was housed in an Orlando fruit-packing warehouse, which had been converted into a skating rink during the icy winter of 1894–5. Leisure attractions have become rather more sophisticated of late (and are rarely as cold), and since the arrival of Walt Disney World, Orlando has been the undisputed gateway to theme park heaven.

Though it is easy for theme park addicts not to venture further afield, visitors in need of a reality check will find that central Florida has much more to offer. Sporting opportunities and state preserves abound, and there are country towns and beach resorts an easy day trip away.

An hour's drive east of Orlando, sea turtles nest on the beach in the shadow of the Kennedy Space Center, one of the state's top attractions. To the west, the cities of St Petersburg and Tampa offer an irresistible combination of notable sightseeing attractions and superb beaches.

> *'Central Florida – a study in reality suspension, brought to your imagination by the nation's finest fantasy makers.'*
>
> FLORIDA TOURIST BOARD

The dolphin statue in Sarasota's marina complex

A Walk Around Bok Tower Gardens

Distance
¾ mile

Time
1½ hours with plenty of stops

Start/end point
Bok Tower Gardens
✚ 29E3
✉ CR17-A, 3 miles N of
Lake Wales
☎ 863/676 1408
🕐 Daily 8–6
♿ Good
🅿 Moderate

Lunch
Garden Restaurant (£)
✉ Bok Tower Gardens
☎ 863/676 1408

*The famous tower,
rising out of lovely
woodland gardens*

These lovely woodland gardens make a relaxing break all year, but they are at the height of their beauty during the cooler winter and spring months. The gardens were founded by Dutch immigrant and philanthropist Edward Bok in the 1920s, and formally opened at a dedication ceremony attended by President Calvin Coolidge in 1929.

From the Visitor Center, take the path that leads up past the dedication plaque and around the White Garden to the Carillon Tower.

The 205ft tower, built of Georgia marble and coquina rock, is adorned with art deco carvings depicting Florida wildlife, and houses the famous 57-bell carillon. Listen out for the clock chimes every half hour, and try to time your visit to coincide with the daily recital at 3PM.

Walk around behind the Carillon Tower to reach the Sunset Overlook.

The Overlook sits at the modest peak of Iron Mountain (298ft), the highest point on the Florida peninsula.

Continue downhill and into the woods on North Walk.

Beneath hanging curtains of Spanish moss, camellias (Nov–Mar), azaleas (Dec–Apr) and other flowering trees and shrubs fill the woodlands with colour. Off Mockingbird Walk, Pinewood House and Gardens are open for occasional tours (telephone for details). The romantic Mediterranean Revival-style house was built in 1931 and sits in 7 acres of picturesque gardens. At the bottom of the hill, on Pine Ridge Trail, there is a birdwatching hide by a small pond. More than 126 bird species have been recorded in the gardens.

Return to the Visitor Center along Woodland Walk.

What to See in Central Florida

BLUE SPRING STATE PARK

This attractive wooded park on the banks of the St Johns River is one of the best places to see wild manatees in central Florida. During the winter months (Nov–Mar), manatees gather here to bask in the warm waters produced from the turquoise blue depths of the park's namesake artesian spring at a constant 72°F. The spring head is a popular swimming hole and dive site. There are also woodland trails, boat trips and kayaks for hire.

CYPRESS GARDENS

Founded in the 1930s, Cypress Gardens is rather sedate as theme parks go, but recently it has made considerable efforts to broaden its appeal. The traditional attractions of a fine lakeside setting, water-ski shows and dazzling horticultural displays have now been augmented with the Nature's Way animal exhibit, the Wings of Wonder butterfly conservatory, concert programmes and night-time laser shows. A highlight, quite literally, is the view from the revolving 153ft Kodak observation platform.

FANTASY OF FLIGHT

A major aviation museum between Orlando and Tampa, Fantasy of Flight combines historic exhibits with state-of-the-art simulator rides. Scale models and authentic aircraft trace the history of flight from the Wright brothers and daredevil antics of 1920s circus barnstormers through to fighter aircraft from World War II and beyond. The Fightertown Flight Simulators put visitors in the hot seat of a B17 Flying Fortress for a stomach-churning mission into enemy territory and an aerial dogfight over the Pacific.

29E4
2100 W French Avenue, Orange City
904/775 3663
Daily 8–sunset
Good
Cheap

Below: *dramatic dioramas at Fantasy of Flight*

29E3
SR540 W, Winter Haven
863/324 2111 or 1-800 282 2123
Daily 9:30–5 (extended summer and hols)
Concessions (£), and restaurant (££)
Very good
Very expensive

29E3
SR559, Polk City
941/984 3500
Daily 9–5 (extended summer and hols)
Compass Rose (£–££)
Good
Moderate (additional charge for Fightertown Flight Simulators)

 29E4

Merritt Island Refuge
 SR406 (4 miles E of
Titusville)
☎ 321/861 0667
⏰ Visitor Center, Mon–Fri
8–4:30, Sat–Sun 9–5.
Closed Sun Feb–Oct

✚ 29F3

Elliott Museum
✉ 825 NE Ocean
Boulevard/A1A
☎ 561/225 1961
⏰ Daily 10–4
♿ Moderate

✚ 29D3
✉ 3708 Patten Avenue
(US301 E), Ellenton
☎ 941/723 4536
⏰ Thu–Mon 9–5; tours 9:30,
10:30, on the hour 1–4
♿ Limited
🎟 Cheap

✚ 29D4
✉ 4150 S Suncoast
Boulevard/US19,
Homosassa
☎ 352/628 5343
⏰ Daily 9–5:30
🍴 Concessions (£)
🎟 Moderate

FLORIDA'S SPACE COAST ✪✪

The big draw here is the terrific Kennedy Space Center
(► 17). Within clear sight of the launch pad, the Space
Coast can also offer the unspoilt dunes of the Canaveral
National Seashore and the marshland wilderness area
protected by **Merritt Island National Wildlife Refuge**. To
the south, the 20-mile strip of barrier island beach between
Cocoa Beach and Melbourne has been developed as a
family resort.

FORT PIERCE ✪

Founded on the site of a Seminole War army outpost, Fort
Pierce's main claims to fame are the barrier beaches of
Hutchinson Island across the Indian River. A favourite spot
for snorkelling is Bathtub Beach, and surfers congregate at
Fort Pierce State Recreation Area or Pepper Beach. Down
near Stuart Beach, the **Elliott Museum** makes an interesting stop. It is named after inventor Sterling Elliott and
contains a variety of historic and eccentric exhibits.

GAMBLE PLANTATION ✪✪✪

The last remaining antebellum house in southern Florida,
this gracious two-storey mansion was built by sugar
planter Major Robert Gamble in the 1840s. Two-foot thick
walls and through breezes help keep the house cool in
summer and the interior has been restored and furnished
with period antiques. At the height of its productivity
around 200 slaves worked Gamble's 3,500-acre plantation,
and tours of the house include many interesting snippets
of information about plantation life.

HOMOSASSA SPRINGS STATE WILDLIFE PARK ✪✪

One of Florida's original natural tourist attractions,
Homosassa Springs is a favourite manatee playground and
showcase for several of the state's other endangered
animal species. An underwater observatory in the 46ft-
deep spring gives an unusual perspective on life in the
Homosassa River, while pontoon boat rides are good for
wildlife-spotting along the riverbank. Look for alligators,
otters and native birds. A variety of Florida black bears, bob
cats and deer can be seen in natural habitat enclosures.

JUNO BEACH MARINELIFE CENTER ✪

Each summer (Jun–Aug), Juno Beach is transformed into a major loggerhead sea turtle nesting ground (► 13). The excellent Marinelife Center has turtle tanks and a turtle nursery, natural history and marine displays, and organises guided beach walks (reservations advised).

✚ 29F2
✉ 14200 US1, Juno Beach
☎ 561/627 8280
🕐 Tue–Sat 10–4, Sun 12–3
💷 Cheap

JUPITER ✪

Once the northern terminus of the 1880s Lake Worth Railroad, which numbered Mars, Venus and Juno among its stops, Jupiter's landmark red lighthouse is hard to miss. It's an offshoot of the Burt Reynolds' Ranch, a strange exercise in hagiography filled with memorabilia. More interesting is the **Florida History Center and Museum**, with collections of Native American and pioneer artefacts.

✚ 29F3

Florida History Center and Museum
✉ 805 N US1
☎ 561/747 6639
🕐 Tue–Fri 10–5, Sat–Sun 12–5
♿ Good

Did you know ?

*Florida manatees (*Trichechus manatus*) are also called sea cows. They are vegetarians and generally grow to between nine and 12 feet, and weigh 1,000 to 2,500 pounds. Their sole enemy is man – but he is formidable enough – and there are only 1,500 to 2,500 manatees left in Florida waters.*

Facing page: *traditional Florida architecture*
Below: *feeding time for the manatees*

In the Know

If you only have a short time to visit Florida, or would like to get a real flavour of the state, here are some ideas:

10
Good Places to Have Lunch

Anthony's (£)
✉ 111 Duval Street, Key West ☎ 305/296 8899. Tasty Greek specialities and terrific salads.
Carmine's (£)
✉ 1802 E 7th Street, Ybor City (Tampa) ☎ 813/248 3834. Mountainous Cuban sandwiches.
Coral Lynn Café (£)
✉ Via de Lela, 240 Worth Avenue, Palm Beach ☎ 561/651 7888. Tasty snacks and salads in a courtyard setting.
Flakowitz Bagel Inn (£)
✉ 1999 N Federal Highway, Boca Raton ☎ 561/368 0666. Bagels

10
Ways to Be a Local

Go fishing – freshwater lakes and streams, beaches, bridges and fishing piers all offer excellent fishing.
Dress down for Florida, the locals are pretty much strangers to formal dress.
Go to a rodeo, one of the rare times Floridians do dress up – in cowboy gear.
Adopt a manatee – manatee rescue operations and refuges are always glad of a donation.
Say 'conk' not 'conch' like a true local (► 6).
Enjoy a margarita on the beach at sunset.
Tipping – do not betray your out-of-state origins by failing to tip.
Tuck into a dolphin – no, not Flipper, the warm-blooded mammal. Dolphin fish is a favourite on Florida seafood menus.
Turn right on red – unless signs say

Above: overhead traffic lights are a common sight

otherwise, drivers in Florida can turn right on a red light (as long as the way is clear, of course).
Send back the Key lime pie if it is green, true Key limes are yellow.

stuffed to bursting point with all manner of goodies.

Lombard's Landing (££)
✉ Universal Studios, Orlando ☎ 407/224 6400. One of Orlando's best theme park restaurants.

Main Squeeze Juice Bar (£)
✉ 105 S 3 Street, Fernandina Beach ☎ 904/277 3003. Cottage with a courtyard for home cooking, beer and wine.

Mr P's Wine and Sandwich Shop (£)
✉ 221 E Zaragoza Street, Pensacola ☎ 850/433 0294. Soups and quiches in the historic district.

News Café (£–££)
✉ 800 Ocean Drive, Miami Beach ☎ 305/538 6397. Omelettes, salads and pasta, with sea view.

The Monk's Vineyard (££)
✉ 56 St George Street, St Augustine ☎ 904/824 5888. Pretty terrace setting for good pub grub.

The Garden Restaurant (£)
✉ 217 Central Avenue, St Petersburg ☎ 727/896 3800. Lunchtime specials include *meze* and pasta.

Top Activities

Birdwatching: Corkscrew Swamp Sanctuary (➤ 41), Merritt Island National Wildlife Refuge (➤ 54), and the Florida Keys are among the top spots.

Boat trips: notable boating areas include the Lee Island Coast (➤ 24), the Everglades (➤ 41), and the Keys (➤ 46).

Canoeing: many riverfront state parks provide canoe trails (➤ 110).

Diving: coral reef diving in the Keys (➤ 46) and fascinating wreck sites off the Emerald Coast (➤ 76, 77).

Fishing: licences are required. Check at bait and tackle shops (➤ 111).

Golf: Florida is one of the world's top golfing destinations with over 1,000 golf courses around the state (➤ 112).

Motorsports: major events at Daytona International Speedway (➤ 74), and Homestead-Miami Speedway (➤ 113).

Polo: a top winter pursuit on the Gold Coast (➤ 113).

Tennis: numerous hotel and public courts (➤ 112).

Watersports: hotels and beachfront concessions rent out windsurfing, sailing, kayaking and dive equipment (➤ 112).

Top Beaches

- Bahia Honda State Recreation Area (➤ 47)
- Caladesi Island State Park (➤ 63)
- Daytona Beach (➤ 74–5)
- Grayton Beach State Recreation Area (➤ 78)
- Kathryn Abbey Hanna State Park (➤ 81)
- Miami Beach (➤ 35)
- Red Reef Park, Boca Raton (➤ 40)
- St Andrews State Recreation Area (➤ 85)
- Sanibel and Captiva Islands (➤ 24)
- Siesta Key, Sarasota (➤ 25)

Below and left: *sunglasses and minimal clothing are the order of the day in Florida*

KENNEDY SPACE CENTER (▶ 17, TOP TEN)

KISSIMMEE ✪

A budget dormitory annexe for Walt Disney World to the south of Orlando, Kissimmee stretches for more than 20 miles along US192 in a seamless strip of hotels, motels, shopping malls and family restaurants. To help visitors find their way around, Navigational Markers (NM) have been posted along the route.

Along the main road (US192), family-style attractions range from miniature golf and fairground rides outside the Old Town Kissimmee shopping mall (▶ 105) to dinner theatres. Out to the west of the I-4 highway, the **Splendid China** theme park features 60 of China's best known scenic, cultural and historic landmarks re-created in amazingly detailed miniature. The half-mile section of the Great Wall of China was constructed from more than eight million tiny bricks. The park also presents live entertainment by Chinese acrobats and dancers.

Just north of Kissimmee, visitors receive a snappy welcome from a pair of outsize alligator jaws at **Gatorland**. This old-fashioned but enduringly popular attraction features hundreds of alligators, 'gator-wrestling shows, educational presentations, an assortment of turtles and snakes, and a boardwalk trail through a marshland alligator breeding ground and bird preserve.

✚ 29E3
🍴 Fast food, cafés/
   restaurants (£–££)

Splendid China
✉ 3000 Splendid China
   Boulevard (NM4.5)
☎ 407/396 7111 or
   1-800 244 6226
🕓 Daily 9:30–7 (extended
   summer and hols)
♿ Very good
💷 Very expensive

Gatorland
✉ 14501 S Orange Blossom
   Trail/US441
☎ 407/855 5496 or
   1-800 393 5297
🕓 Daily 8–dusk
♿ Good
💷 Expensive

*The gaping entrance
to Gatorland*

Thoroughbred horses graze Ocala's rich pastures

MOUNT DORA ⊘

A pretty lakeside country town set in the citrus groves north of Orlando, Mount Dora was founded back in the 1870s. The restored downtown district offers an attractive selection of gift shops, galleries and cafés, there are boat trips and walks around the lake, and the Chamber of Commerce distributes drive tour maps to the town's historic Victorian homes.

✚ 29E4
🍴 Windsor Rose English Tea Room (£–££), 144 W 4th Avenue ☎ 352/735 2551
❓ Drive tour maps from Chamber of Commerce, 341 Alexander Street

OCALA ⊘⊘

The rolling pastures of Marion County are the centre of Florida's billion-dollar horse-breeding industry, bordering the vast pinewood preserve of the Ocala National Forest. Ten miles east of Ocala, the 400,000-acre national forest offers a range of outdoor activities including excellent hiking trails, fishing, boating, swimming and some of the most attractive canoe trails in the state (➤ 110).

On the edge of the forest, glass-bottomed boat rides at **Silver Springs** have been a local sightseeing feature since 1878. The world's largest artesian spring is now part of a theme park attraction with Silver River cruises, exotic animals and Jeep safaris touring the woodlands where the original Tarzan movies were filmed in the 1930s.

✚ 29D4
❓ Details of horse farm visits: Ocala Chamber of Commerce, 110 E Silver Springs Boulevard ☎ 352/629 8051

Silver Springs
✉ 5656 E Silver Springs Boulevard
☎ 352/236 2121
🕐 Daily 10–5 (extended summer and hols)
♿ Limited
✋ Very expensive

ORLANDO ⊘⊘⊘

Launched into the limelight by the opening of Disney's Magic Kingdom in 1971, Orlando is the undisputed world capital of theme parks and a bustling modern city 15 miles north of the Walt Disney World Resort (➤ 70–1). The main tourist area is in the south around International Drive, or I-Drive as it is generally known. It runs parallel to the I-4 highway, which helps cut journey times between the city's widely spread attractions.

The biggest attraction on (or just off) I-Drive is **Universal Orlando**, with its two theme parks and the CityWalk shopping, dining and entertainment district. Universal Studio's top rides include Back to the Future and the interactive MEN IN BLACK Alien Attack, the world's first life-size, ride-through video game. Don't miss the excellent Terminator 2: 3-D show and things get pretty wild in the hurricane zone at Twister.

✚ 29E4
🍴 Fast food, cafés, restaurants (£–£££)
🚌 I-Ride service along International Drive between Belz Factory Mall and SeaWorld

Universal Orlando
✚ 60B2
✉ 1000 Universal Studios Plaza
☎ 407/363 8000 or 1-888 837 2273
🕐 Daily
♿ Very good
✋ Very expensive

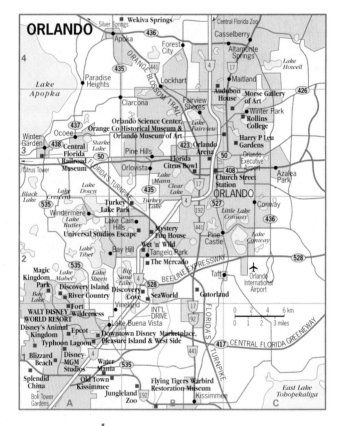

ORLANDO

SeaWorld Orlando

📍 60B2

✉ 7007 SeaWorld Drive

☎ 407/351 3600 or 1-800 327 2424

🕐 Daily 9–7 (extended summer and hols)

🍴 Concessions, cafés and family restaurants (£–£££)

🚌 I-Ride, Lynx 42

♿ Very good

💰 Very expensive

Unveiled in 1999, Universal's second park, Islands of Adventure, is a homage to the comicstrip. Guests receive a ticket to ride the cartoons from the heights of the Incredible Hulk Roller Coaster and Doctor Doom's Fearfall to the depths of Popeye and Bluto's Bilge-Rat Barges raft ride. The world's most technologically advanced theme park (allegedly) is also the place to get to grips with the brilliant robotic models of Jurassic Park, the fantasy world of the Lost Continent and the whimsical Seuss Landing.

Heading south of I-Drive, **SeaWorld** is Orlando's other major theme park. The world's most popular marine park offers a full day of entertaining shows starring killer whales, dolphins, sea lions and more. In between the shows, there are fantastic aquarium displays, the

enchanting Penguin Encounter, manatees, touch tanks, polar bears and beluga whales as well as the Kraken roller-coaster and Journey To Atlantis thrill ride. SeaWorld's sister park, **Discovery Cove**, specialises in interactive marine adventures. Park admission is restricted to 1,000 visitors a day and the lucky few can experience a raft of water-based activities including snorkelling in the Coral Reef pool and swimming with bottlenose dolphins.

Downtown Orlando rises in a miniature forest of mirrored glass towers on the shores of Lake Eola. In its shadow, a restored historic district is home to the lively Church Street Station shopping, dining and entertainment complex (➤ 105). The area has also attracted a wide choice of restaurants and bars.

To the north, the terrific **Orlando Science Center** is one of the best science museums in the state. Laid out on four levels beneath a landmark silver observatory dome, the museum is packed with dozens of eye-catching and entertaining interactive exhibits, Florida habitat displays, movie special effects demonstrations and a planetarium.

Near by, the gorgeous **Harry P Leu Gardens** offer gentle strolls on the banks of Lake Rowena and impressive formal rose gardens. In springtime the magnolias burst into colour with a spectacular show of camellias planted by the Leus, who lived at the heart of the gardens. Their much enlarged pioneer home is open for tours.

The pretty northeastern suburb of Winter Park also makes a delightful escape from the crowds. There is upscale shopping on Park Avenue, boat trips on Lake Osceola, and a superb collection of Tiffany glassware and art nouveau at the Morse Gallery of Art.

Discovery Cove
- ✚ 60B2
- ✉ 6000 Discovery Cove Way
- ☎ 407/370 1280 or 1-800 327 2424
- ◷ Daily (check schedules)
- 🍴 Very expensive

Orlando Science Center
- ✚ 60B/C3
- ✉ 777 E Princeton Street
- ☎ 407/514 2000 or 1-800 672 4386
- ◷ Mon–Thu 9–5, Fri–Sat 9–9, Sun 12–5
- ♿ Very good
- 🍴 Moderate

Harry P Leu Gardens
- ✚ 60C3
- ✉ 1920 N Forest Avenue
- ☎ 407/246 2620
- ◷ Daily 9–5
- ♿ Good
- 🍴 Moderate
- ❓ Leu House tours, Tue–Sat 10–3:30, Sun–Mon 1–3:30

Above and below: *historic Church Street Station*

North of Orlando

Distance
120 miles (plus 20 for the detour)

Time
8 hours with stops

Start/end point
Orlando
✚ 29E4

Lunch
Take a picnic to Ocala National Forest. Concession stand (£) only at Juniper Springs

This day trip covers three diverse central Florida sights.

From Orlando, take SR50 west to Clermont (22 miles), then north on US27 to Lakeridge Winery and Vineyards (6 miles).

Surrounded by fields striped with rows of vines, a Visitor Center offers guided tours of the winery followed by free tastings of red, white and sparkling wines.

Continue north on US27 to SR19 N (3 miles). Follow SR19 north all the way to the Ocala National Forest (30 miles). The southern Visitor Center is just inside the forest on the left.

Drop in at the Visitor Center to pick up maps and brochures giving details of the national forest's numerous outdoor attractions (▶ 59). One of the nicest spots is the Juniper Springs Recreation Area.

An enticing array of shops line Mount Dora's quiet streets

To reach Juniper Springs, keep north on SR19 to SR40, then turn left (west). The entrance is on the right. Take SR19 south for a direct route to Mount Dora. For a more scenic detour, keep west on SR40 to CR314-A, turn left and follow the forest road south. Two miles beyond CR464, turn right on to SE 182nd Av Road (by a corner store). At CR42 (7 ½ miles) turn left, then right (1 mile) still on CR42 for Eustis (11 miles), and pick up signs for Mount Dora (9 miles).

Renowned for its genteel Victorian architecture, speciality shopping, and tempting tea shops, Mount Dora is a charming place to stop for a break (▶ 59).

Take 5th Avenue to Old 441 South, which joins US441 (3 miles), the road back to Orlando (20 miles).

PINELLAS SUNCOAST

A 28-mile strip of hotel-lined barrier island beaches, the Pinellas Suncoast is the busiest resort area on the Gulf coast. The two liveliest districts are St Pete Beach in the south, and Clearwater Beach in the north, both of which make good seaside bases for trips around the Tampa Bay area. From Clearwater Beach, there are boat services to gorgeous Caladesi Island, a barrier island preserve with one of the finest beaches in the country.

The area has a couple of low-key attractions, the best of which is the **Pinellas County Heritage Village**, a collection of 23 carefully restored historic buildings. Pioneer cabins, Edwardian homes, a church and a train station are among the exhibits. Another popular stop is the Suncoast Seabird Sanctuary, which rescues and rehabilitates pelicans, herons, egrets and other birds.

66A3
Cafés/restaurants (£–£££)
St Petersburg (➤ 23), Sarasota (➤ 25), Tampa (➤ below)

Pinellas County Heritage Village
✉ 11909 125th Street N, Largo
☎ 727/582 2123
🕐 Tue–Sat 10–4, Sun 1–4
♿ Good
Free

ST PETERSBURG (➤ 23, TOP TEN)

SARASOTA (➤ 25, TOP TEN)

TAMPA

A buzzing bayfront city, Tampa boasts some of the most varied and exciting attractions on the Gulf coast. Henry Plant brought the railroad to town in 1884 and built a grand hotel to house the expected flood of tourists. The city's prospects improved further with the arrival of Cuban cigar workers in 1886, who established themselves at Ybor City. Plant's lavish Moorish Revival-style hotel is a local landmark. Its silver onion-domed minarets act as a beacon for visitors crossing the Hillsborough River from downtown to look around the **Henry B Plant Museum** housed in a suite of former hotel rooms.

Pelicans ready for lunch at Suncoast Seabird Sanctuary

29D3
Cafés/restaurants (£–£££)
Lowry Park Zoo (➤ 109), St Petersburg (➤ 23)

Henry B Plant Museum
✉ 401 W JF Kennedy Boulevard
☎ 813/254 1891
🕐 Tue–Sat 10–4, Sun 12–4
♿ Good
Donations

Tampa Museum of Art
 600 N Ashley Drive
☎ 813/274 8130
🕐 Tue–Sat 10–5 (Thu until 8), Sun 1–5
♿ Very good
💲 Cheap

Florida Aquarium
✉ 701 Channelside Drive
☎ 813/273 4020
🕐 Daily 9:30–5
♿ Very good
💲 Expensive

Busch Gardens
✉ 3000 E Busch Boulevard (at 40th Street)
☎ 813/987 5082
🕐 Daily 9:30–6 (extended summer and hols)
♿ Good
💲 Very expensive

Museum of Science and Industry (MOSI)
✉ 4801 E Fowler Avenue
☎ 813/987 6100
🕐 Daily from 9AM
♿ Very good
💲 Expensive

Downtown Tampa is compact and easy to explore on foot. Backing on to the river, the **Tampa Museum of Art** displays fine collections of Greek and Roman antiquities and 20th-century American art, shown in rotation, and hosts interesting travelling exhibitions.

Down on the waterfront, the terrific **Florida Aquarium** should not be missed. Displays follow a drop of water from the Florida aquifer on its journey to the sea via river and swamp dioramas inhabited by live waterbirds, otters and freshwater fish. There are scurrying crabs in Bays and Beaches, a Coral Reef exhibit with dive demonstrations, and Offshore tanks showcasing local marine life.

Out to the east of the city, Tampa's top crowd-puller is the huge African-inspired **Busch Gardens** theme park, which doubles as one of the nation's premier zoos. More than 3,300 animals roam the central 160-acre Serengeti Plain and appear in special exhibits such as the Great Ape Domain and the Edge of Africa safari experience. Busch Gardens is also famous for its thrill rides including Montu, one of the world's tallest and longest inverted roller-coasters, and the spectacular Tanganyika Tidal Wave.

Just down the road from Busch Gardens, the **Museum of Science and Industry** (generally referred to as MOSI) inhabits a striking modern architectural complex. Here, imaginative interactive displays tackle the mysteries of the world about us and the GTE Challenger Learning Center turns the spotlight on to space travel and research.

Roller-coaster fans experience Montu, the top thrill ride at Busch Gardens

A Walk Around Ybor City

Tampa's historic cigar-making quarter has undergone a modest renaissance. Old cigar factories and workers' cottages now house shops, cafés and restaurants, and the weekend club scene is hugely popular. The starting point is Ybor Square, the original red-brick cigar factory, which has been transformed into a shopping mall.

Turn left out of the front entrance on to Avenida Republica de Cuba for a short walk to the corner of 9th Avenue.

On the opposite corner are the arcades of the old Cherokee Club, once patronised by Cuban freedom fighter José Martí, Teddy Roosevelt and Winston Churchill.

Turn right for one block on 9th, leading directly to the Ybor City State Museum. It is more fun to walk down 15th Street and along 7th Avenue, or La Septima, Ybor City's main shopping street. Cut back up to 9th Avenue at 18th Street; turn right.

The museum displays tell the story of the cigar industry and the various migrant groups who came to work here. Down the street, a worker's 'shotgun' cottage has been restored.

Cut across the plaza by the Immigrant Statue to 19th Street. Rejoin 7th Avenue, and turn left.

The walk-in humidor at Arturo Fuente Cigars, number 2014, is one of several interesting stops along this section of La Septima. The Columbia Restaurant building, on the corner of 21st Street, is lavishly adorned with hand-painted tiles.

Walk back down 7th Avenue with its fashion stores, design emporiums and gift shops.

Distance
1½ miles

Time
2 hours with stops

Start/end point
Ybor Square
✚ 67E4
🚌 8, 46

Lunch
Little Sicily (£)
✉ 1724 8th Avenue E (at 18th Street)
☎ 813/248 2940

Did you know ?
The name Tampa means 'sticks of fire', and around 500 million cigars are produced in the city each year. Annual sales are in the region of $150 million.

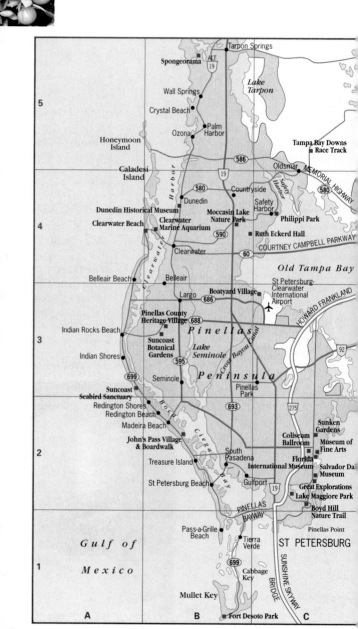

Tarpon Springs
Spongeorama
ALT 19
Lake
Tarpon
Wall Springs
Crystal Beach
Ozona
Palm
Harbor
Honeymoon
Island
Tampa Bay Downs
Race Track
586
Caladesi
Island
19
Oldsmar
MEMORIAL HIGHWAY
580
580
Countryside
Safety
Harbor
Safety
Harbor
Dunedin Historical Museum
Dunedin
Moccasin Lake
Nature Park
Philippi Park
Clearwater Beach
Clearwater
Marine Aquarium
590
Ruth Eckerd Hall
60
COURTNEY CAMPBELL PARKWAY
Clearwater
Old Tampa Bay
Belleair Beach
Belleair
St Petersburg-
Clearwater
International
Airport
HOWARD FRANKLAND
Largo
Boatyard Village
686
92
Pinellas County
Heritage Village
688
Pinellas
Indian Rocks Beach
Suncoast
Botanical
Gardens
595
Lake
Seminole
Peninsula
Indian Shores
699
Seminole
Pinellas
Park
Suncoast
Seabird Sanctuary
693
275
Redington Shores
Redington Beach
Sunken
Gardens
Madeira Beach
Coliseum
Ballroom
Museum of
Fine Arts
John's Pass Village
& Boardwalk
South
Pasadena
Florida
International Museum
Salvador Da
Museum
Treasure Island
Great Explorations
St Petersburg Beach
Gulfport
19
Lake Maggiore Park
Boyd Hill
Nature Trail
PINELLAS
BAYWAY
Pinellas Point
ST PETERSBURG
Pass-a-Grille
Beach
Tierra
Verde
Gulf of
Mexico
699
SUNSHINE SKYWAY
Cabbage
Key
BRIDGE
Mullet Key
Fort Desoto Park
5
4
3
2
1
A
B
C

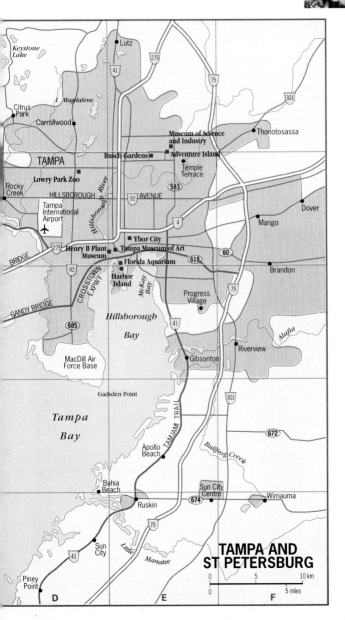

Keystone
Lake

Lutz

275

41

75

301

Citrus
Park

L. Magdalene

Carrollwood

Thonotosassa

Museum of Science
and Industry

TAMPA

Busch Gardens ■

■ Adventure Island

Temple
Terrace

Lowry Park Zoo ■

Rocky
Creek

HILLSBOROUGH

92

AVENUE

583

Dover

4

Mango

Tampa
International
Airport

✈

Hillsborough River

Ybor City ■

275

Henry B Plant ■
Museum

■ Tampa Museum of Art

60

BRIDGE

92

■ Florida Aquarium

618

Brandon

Harbor
Island ■

75

CROSSTOWN EXPWY

McKay
Bay

Progress
Village

GANDY BRIDGE

685

Hillsborough

Bay

41

Alafia

MacDill Air
Force Base

Riverview

Gibsonton ■

Gadsden Point

301

672

TAMIAMI TRAIL

Tampa
Bay

Bullfrog Creek

Apollo
Beach

Bahia
Beach

Sun City
Centre ■

674

■ Wimauma

Ruskin

75

41

Sun
City

Little

Manatee

TAMPA AND
ST PETERSBURG

0   5   10 km

0   5 miles

Piney
Point

D   E   F

67

Around Tampa Bay

Distance
125 miles

Time
8 hours including stops

Start/end point
St Petersburg
✚ 66C2

Lunch
Banyan Café (£)
✉ Ringling Museum
☎ 941/359 3181

The Sunshine Skyway Bridge spans Tampa Bay

The start point for this day trip around Tampa Bay is downtown St Petersburg.

Take 4th Street/US92 north and east across Gandy Bridge to connect with the Tampa's Crosstown Expressway. The Florida Aquarium exit is 6B.

The $84-million state-of-the-art Florida Aquarium makes a fascinating interlude (➤ 64).

Rejoin the Expressway heading east (direction Brandon), to Exit 15–A. Take I-75 south (direction Naples) to Exit 43 (30 miles). Turn on to US301 south for 1 mile to Ellenton for the Gamble Plantation.

The historic Gamble mansion is a fine example of mid-19th-century antebellum architecture (➤ 54).

Rejoin I-75 south to Exit 40 (12 miles), and follow University Parkway right to the gates of the Ringling Museum (7 miles) in Sarasota.

Circus king John Ringling's magnificent winter home and estate overlook Sarasota Bay (➤ 25).

From the Ringling Museum, US41 heads north to connect with US19, the direct route to the Sunshine Skyway bridge and St Petersburg (40 miles). If you have time and fancy a swim, turn south on US41 for 3 miles, bear right for St Armands Key (SR789 N), and cross the John Ringling Causeway. Keep right following SR789 N along the barrier island beaches.

A recommended place to stop here is Bradenton Beach, which has an attractive strip of cafés, shops and water-sports concessions facing the Gulf.

SR64 leads back to US41 at Bradenton.

The 4-mile Sunshine Skyway is quite an attraction in its own right. Dedicated in 1987, it has a record 1,200ft main span rising 175ft above the entrance to Tampa Bay.

TARPON SPRINGS ✪

A little piece of Florida that is forever Greek, the sponge fishing centre of Tarpon Springs has a distinctly Mediterranean air. Greek divers first came here to harvest the Gulf sponge beds in the early 1900s. As well as their sponging skills they imported a hefty slice of Greek culture, which has turned the dockside town into something of a tourist magnet.

Piles of sponges decorate Dodecanese Boulevard, the bustling main thoroughfare, where sidewalk cafés play bouzouki music and sell ouzo. Join one of the narrated boat trips around the docks for a lesson in local history, and drop in on the **Tarpon Springs Aquarium** for a peek at local marine life. For scrumptious treats, be sure to sample the delicious sweet and savoury Greek pastries on offer in a host of bakeries.

VERO BEACH ✪

Chosen by Disney for their first Florida seaside resort, Vero Beach has a reputation for lovely holiday homes, a celebrated arts centre, and muted luxury. Galleries and boutiques gather on Ocean Drive, near the landmark Driftwood Resort. This eccentric oceanfront property was founded in the 1930s, and is partially constructed from timber washed ashore on the beach.

North of town, along the Treasure Coast, the **Sebastian Inlet State Recreation Area** is a favourite with surfers and fishermen. The McLarty Treasure Museum describes how the Treasure Coast got its name when the Spanish Plate Fleet was dashed on to the reefs during a storm in 1715.

Natural sponges for sale at Tarpon Springs

✚ 66B5
🍴 Cafés/restaurants (£–£££)

Tarpon Springs Aquarium
✉ 850 Dodecanese Boulevard
☎ 727/938 5378
🕐 Daily 10–5
♿ Good
✋ Cheap

✚ 29F3
🍴 Cafés/restaurants (£–£££)

Sebastian Inlet State Recreation Area
✉ 9700 S A1A
☎ 321/984 4852
🕐 Daily 8–dusk
♿ Good
✋ Cheap

The Driftwood Inn at Vero Beach

 60A1

✉ Lake Buena Vista (20 miles south of Orlando)

☎ Information: 407/824 4321; reservations: 407/934 7639

🕐 Check current schedules

🍴 Each park offers a choice throughout the day. Make reservations at Guest Relations for table service restaurants (££–£££)

🚌 Free bus from many Orlando/Kissimmee hotels. Walt Disney World transport operates from the Magic Kingdom ticketing centre

♿ Excellent

💲 Very expensive

❓ Details of daily parades, shows, fireworks and laser displays are in park guides

Above: *Countdown to Extinction in Disney's Animal Kingdom*

Fastpass
Beat the queues with the time-saving Disney FASTPASS designed to cut waiting times on the most popular rides in all four parks. Insert your admission ticket into the FASTPASS machines at the rides offering the complimentary service and you'll receive a designated ride time.

WALT DISNEY WORLD RESORT ✪✪✪

Walt Disney World (➤ 26) is truly a world within a world. The biggest entertainment complex on the planet boasts four theme parks, three water parks and enough shopping, dining, and nightlife to keep the family entertained full time. Around 23 million guests visit Walt Disney World annually, and it can get extremely busy. Avoid holiday periods if you can; the most comfortable times to visit, both on the crowd and the weather front, are mid-September until mid-December, and January until mid-February. The Disney experience does not come cheap, but tickets (➤ panel opposite) can be purchased ahead, which helps with budget planning as well as cutting down on queuing at the gates; reservations for accommodation should be made well in advance.

The following is a *very* brief guide to the best that Walt Disney World has to offer.

Disney's Animal Kingdom The newest and largest of the Disney theme parks (five times bigger than the Magic Kingdom) opened in the spring of 1998. The giant 14-storey Tree of Life towers over Safari Village at the heart of the park, linked by bridges to Africa, Asia, DinoLand U.S.A. and the small child-friendly Camp Minnie-Mickey. Top rides include Kilimanjaro Safaris into the 100-acre African savannah for close encounters with exotic animals and in DinoLand U.S.A. the dramatic dinosaur adventure.

Disney-MGM Studios A fun Hollywood-style setting for rides and shows culled from Disney's favourite movies. The Backlot Tour, Backstage Pass and Magic of Disney Animation step behind the scenes of the studio, while shows highlight blockbuster successes such as *The Little Mermaid* and *Beauty and the Beast*. The best thrill rides are Twilight Zone™ Tower of Terror, the Rock 'n' Roller Coaster and Star Tours.

Downtown Disney Marketplace, Pleasure Island and West Side A mega entertainment district on the shores of Lake Buena Vista, Downtown Disney encompasses shopping, celebrity restaurants and entertainments. The new Disney West Side attractions include a giant cinema complex and theatre, while the Pleasure Island nightlife zone has no fewer than eight clubs, which run the gamut from 1970s disco hits to country music.

Epcot A park in two parts, Disney's Experimental Prototype Community of Tomorrow looks at the world about us. Future World tackles things scientific with typical Disney flair. Highlights include the Living Seas aquarium, the boat ride through experimental gardens in The Land, the brilliant dinosaur romp in Universe of Energy and Spaceship Earth. World Showcase presents 11 pavilions, set around the Lagoon, depicting the potted architecture and culture of nations as diverse as Canada and China.

MAGIC KINGDOM (► 26, TOP TEN)

Water Parks Disney's three water parks are enormously popular for a day away from the theme park trail. The biggest and arguably the best is Blizzard Beach with its bizarre ski resort theme and mountainous water slides. Typhoon Lagoon goes for the shipwrecked tropical look, a huge wave-pool lagoon and rafting adventures. River Country is a Huck Finn-style swimming hole on Bay Lake.

WEEKI WACHEE SPRINGS WATERPARK ✪
One of those truly weird 'only in Florida' attractions, this veteran theme park's unique selling point is its underwater ballets performed by live 'mermaids'. For students of the kitsch it is a must. Less unusual attractions include a wilderness river cruise, a water park with waterslides, riverfront picnic area and sandy beach.

Ticket Options

For short-stay visitors, the only ticket option available is one-day one-park tickets. For longer stay visitors, and those planning to return either later in the holiday or years hence, 5 and 7 Day Park Hopper Plus Passes offer unbeatable flexibility, plus savings on single day tickets. The Passes cover unlimited admission to all four theme parks and a choice of entries to the water parks, Pleasure Island and Disney's Wide World of Sport. Pass-holders are free to hop from park to park on the same day and use the transportation system, and unused days never expire.

Above: *the monorail glides past Spaceship Earth in Future World*

✚ 29D4
✉ US19 at SR 50
☎ 352/596 2062 or 1-800 678 9335
🕐 Daily 9:30–5:30
🍴 Mermaid Gallery (£)
💲 Expensive

71

Northern Florida

Northern Florida is the cradle of the state, where 16th-century Spanish explorers, pioneer adventurers and plantation owners put down roots long before the advent of the railroad. Bordered by Georgia and Alabama, the north has a distinctly Old South feel, particularly in the Panhandle, where attitudes are more old-fashioned and antebellum architecture nestles beneath giant live oaks.

Between Pensacola and the fishing villages and marshlands of the Big Bend, the Panhandle's blinding quartz sand beaches are the most spectacular in the state. Inland are glassy clear streams and rivers, such as the famous Suwannee.

The other face of the north is the First Coast, which unfurls along the Atlantic shore between the strikingly dissimilar resorts of cosy Fernandina Beach, historic St Augustine, and bold-as-brass Daytona – all easily reached from Orlando.

> *' Way down upon de*
> *Swanee ribber,*
> *Far, far away,*
> *Dere's wha' my heart is*
> *turning ebber,*
> *Dere's wha' de old folks*
> *stay. '*

STEPHEN C FOSTER
Old Folks at Home (1851)

————————●————————

A Daytona life-guard mans his beach station

What to See in Northern Florida

APALACHICOLA

✚ 28C5
🍴 Cafés/restaurants (£–£££)
❓ Walking tour maps available from the Chamber of Commerce, 99 Market Street, Suite 100. Florida Seafood Festival, first weekend in Nov

Florida's premier oyster producer, this delightful small town lies at the mouth of the Apalachicola River, which feeds the nutrient-rich oyster beds in the bay. Down by the docks, the old brick cotton warehouses stand testament to Apalachicola's days as a thriving 19th-century customs post, and around town there are dozens of gracious old homes built by successful merchants. There is no beach, but St George Island has a beautiful strip of barrier island shore across the causeway from Eastpoint.

CEDAR KEY ⊗⊗

✚ 29D4
🍴 Cafés/restaurants (£–££)

Manatee Springs State Park
✉ SR320 (6 miles W of Chiefland)
☎ 352/493 6072
🕐 Daily 8–dusk
✋ Cheap

At the southern extent of the Big Bend, where the Panhandle meets the Florida peninsula, this quirky and weatherbeaten fishing village looks out over the Gulf of Mexico from the tail end of a string of tiny island keys. It is a laid-back retreat for fishermen and birdwatchers with boat trips, seafood restaurants, and a funny little museum telling the story of the 19th-century logging boom that cleared the namesake cedar forests.

This is also a good base for trips to **Manatee Springs State Park**, a favourite wintering spot for manatees, with hiking paths and canoe trails on the Suwannee River.

DAYTONA ⊗⊗⊗

✚ 29E4
🍴 Cafés/restaurants (£–£££)
❓ Speedweeks/Daytona 500, Feb; Bike Week, Mar; Biketoberfest, Oct

DAYTONA USA
✉ 1801 W International Speedway Boulevard
☎ 904/947 6800
🕐 Daily 9–6
♿ Very good
✋ Expensive

Daytona's love affair with the combustion engine dates back to the early 1900s, when the likes of Henry Ford, Louis Chevrolet and Harvey Firestone flocked south to enjoy the winter sunshine. Today, the 'World Center of Racing' divides its attractions between the hotel-lined sands of Daytona Beach and mainland Daytona across the Halifax River.

Daytona Beach's chief attraction is the broad sandy shore, which is fully geared up for watersports and old-time family fun. There are amusement arcades, fishing, dining and aerial gondola rides on Ocean Pier, candy floss and go-karts on The Boardwalk, and an open-air bandshell. A rather bizarre selling

Daytona International Speedway is a must for race fans

point is that you can park your car on the beach.

On the mainland, the biggest crowd-puller is Daytona International Speedway, home of the Daytona 500 and a state-of-the-art visitor centre, **DAYTONA USA**. This is petrolhead heaven with a range of interactive racing-themed exhibits, loads of memorabilia, a behind-the-scenes racing movie, and track tours on non-race days. Auto fans will also like the **Klassix Auto Attraction** with its collections of classic and vintage cars and bikes, and a complete series of Corvettes from 1953 onwards.

The **Museum of Arts and Sciences** has something for everyone. Children love the 130,000-year-old giant sloth skeleton and 'hands-on' artefacts; there is also a superb collection of fine and decorative American arts and crafts in the Dow Gallery, plus a notable Cuban Museum, spotlighting Latin American culture from 1759 to 1959.

South of Daytona Beach, the **Ponce Inlet Lighthouse Museum** is a popular outing. Built in 1887, the 175ft tower affords far-reaching views along the coast. Down below, the old keeper's quarters display historical and nautical exhibits, and a special building houses a superb 17ft-tall first order Fresnel lens, which resembles an enormous glass and brass pine cone.

Klassix Auto Attraction
- ✉ 2909 W International Speedway Boulevard
- ☎ 904/252 3800
- 🕐 Daily 9–6
- 👤 Moderate

Museum of Arts and Sciences
- ✉ 1040 Museum Boulevard
- ☎ 904/255 0285
- 🕐 Tue–Fri 9–4, Sat–Sun 12–5
- 👤 Cheap

Ponce Inlet Lighthouse Museum
- ✉ 4931 S Peninsula Drive
- ☎ 904/761 1821
- 🕐 Daily 10–4
- 👤 Cheap

Did you know ?

Alexander Winton set the first land speed record on Daytona Beach in 1903. He was clocked at 68mph. Thirty–two years later Malcolm Campbell reached 276mph while setting the last world speed record to be established on the beach.

🕇 28B5
🍴 Cafés/restaurants (£–££)
❓ Destin Fishing Rodeo and
Seafood Festival, Oct

Above: *each building
has a unique charm in
Fernandina Beach*

🕇 28B5
✉ SR395, Port Washington
☎ 850/231 4214
🕐 Gardens, daily 8–dusk;
house, guided tours
Thu–Mon 9–4
💰 Gardens, free; house,
cheap

🕇 29E5
🍴 Cafés/restaurants (£–£££)
❓ Historic district walking
tours from Amelia Island
Museum of History
(opposite)

DESTIN ✪
Destin revels in the title of the 'World's Luckiest Fishing
Village'. At the eastern end of the Emerald Coast, where
the Gulf waters are indeed an incredible green, local
marinas harbour the largest fleet of charter fishing boats in
Florida, and trophy catches include blue marlin, tarpon and
wahoo. If putting out to sea in boats is not your thing,
there is still the opportunity to impress – sizeable tarpon
have been hooked off the 1,200ft Okaloosa Pier.

EDEN STATE GARDENS AND MANSION ✪✪
This lovely antebellum-style mansion was built on the
banks of the Choctawhatchee River by logging baron
William H Wesley in 1897. The house has been meticu-
lously restored and furnished with antiques. Outside,
shaded by towering southern magnolias and live oaks
draped with Spanish moss, the lawned gardens lead down
to the water, where picnickers are welcome on the
riverbank. One of the best times to visit is in spring, when
the azaleas and camellias are in flower.

FERNANDINA BEACH ✪✪✪
At the northern corner of Amelia Island, facing Georgia
across the St Mary's River, Fernandina is a charming small
resort and fishing centre famous for its 50-block Victorian
Historic District.

At the heart of town, Centre Street leads down to the
wharves, where the shrimping fleet docks. Quiet streets
are lined with a veritable lexicon of Victorian architectural

Amelia Island Museum of History
- ✉ 233 S 3rd Street
- ☎ 904/261 7378
- ⏰ Mon–Sat for tours at 11 and 2
- ♿ Good
- 💷 Cheap

Fort Clinch State Park
- ✉ 2601 Atlantic Avenue
- ☎ 904/277 7274
- ⏰ Daily 8–dusk
- 💷 Cheap

styles from Queen Anne homes and Italianate villas to ornate Chinese Chippendale creations built by logging barons and sea captains. Many of these are now bed and breakfast inns, and there are several luxurious resorts on the island.

Fernandina's chequered past is unravelled in the **Amelia Island Museum of History**. This strategic site has been fought over so many times it is known as the Isle of Eight Flags, and oral history tours of the museum are illustrated with centuries-old Timucua Indian artefacts and Spanish colonial relics. There is more history in store at **Fort Clinch State Park** where rangers adopt Civil War uniforms and take part in monthly historic re-enactments. In the grounds surrounding the massive 19th-century brick fort there are hiking trails, beaches and a campsite.

Below: *sea lion shows are popular with visitors*

FORT WALTON ✪

The western anchor of the Emerald Coast, which stretches east in a 24-mile swathe of dazzling quartz sand to Destin (► 76), Fort Walton is a well-developed family resort with affordable accommodation, very safe swimming, watersports, fishing and golf. As well as the glories of the beach, there is marine life entertainment at the **Gulfarium**. Regular dolphin and sea lion shows are interspersed by aquarium displays, the Living Sea exhibit with its sharks and sea turtles, free-ranging exotic birds and enclosures for alligators and 600-pound grey seals.

North of the town, across Choctawhatchee Bay, the enormous Eglin Air Force Base welcomes visitors to the **US Air Force Armament Museum**, the only museum in the US dedicated to Air Force weaponry. Top exhibits include an SR-71 'Blackbird' spy plane, and there are free tours of the 720-square mile base, the largest air force base in the world, which also controls a 86,500-square mile flight test area above the Gulf of Mexico.

- ✉ 28B5
- 🍴 Cafés/restaurants (£–£££)

Gulfarium
- ✉ 1010 Miracle Strip Parkway/US98 E
- ☎ 850/243 9046
- ⏰ Daily, Jun–Sep 9–6; Oct–May 9–4
- 💷 Expensive

US Air Force Armament Museum
- ✉ 100 Museum Drive/ SR85, Shalimar
- ☎ 850/882 4062
- ⏰ Daily 9:30–4:30
- 💷 Free

29D5

Florida Museum of Natural History
 Hull Road (off SW 34th Street)
☎ 352/846 2000
⏱ Mon–Sat 9–5, Sun and holidays 1–5
♿ Very good
✋ Free

Samuel P Harn Museum of Art
✉ Hull Road
☎ 352/392 9826
⏱ Tue–Thu 11–5, Sat 10–5, Sun 1–5
♿ Very good
✋ Free

Fine art adorns the galleries at the Samuel P Harn Museum

✚ 28B5
🍴 Limited options (£–£££)

Grayton Beach State Recreation Area
✉ CR30–A (off US98)
☎ 850/231 4210
⏱ Daily 8–dusk
✋ Cheap

GAINESVILLE ✪✪

A pleasantly leafy university town, Gainesville is home to the University of Florida and its mighty Gators American football team. Football weekends are to be avoided unless you are a fan, but otherwise head for the campus, where two of Gainesville's highlights are to be found.

First stop is the excellent **Florida Museum of Natural History**, which covers both the history and geography of the state. The Florida Heritage section is particularly good value, and children adore the prehistoric skeletons and the thousands of 'hands-on' artefacts in the Object Gallery.

The neighbouring and highly regarded **Samuel P Harn Museum of Art** is another campus crown jewel with impressive collections of ancient and modern arts and crafts from Europe, Asia, Africa and South America as well as the Chandler Collection of American Art. The collections have to be shown in rotation, and they frequently make way for high-profile travelling exhibitions.

Southwest of the town, the Kanapaha Botanical Gardens are a tranquil spot, with a hummingbird garden and woodland paths where spring flowers, azaleas and camellias bloom early in the year. In summer, giant Amazon water lily pads float on the lake like 5ft-wide tea trays, and a tangle of honeysuckle, clematis, passion flowers and jasmine wreathes the arches of the fragrant vinery.

Another interesting side trip is the Devil's Millhopper State Geological Site. The 500ft-wide natural sinkhole was caused by the collapse of the thin limestone crust covering an underground cavern. A 232-step staircase winds down into its cool 120ft-deep fern flanked recesses, which are watered by a dozen miniature waterfalls.

GRAYTON BEACH ✪

A rare low-key seaside enclave on the Panhandle shore, with pine-shaded family holiday homes fronted by a magnificent stretch of beach. Preserved by the **Grayton Beach State Recreation Area**, it is often ranked in the top ten beaches in the US.

Just east of town, the whimsical Old Florida-style resort of Seaside is a local

landmark and tourist attraction. Ostentatiously cute Victorian-inspired cottages with gingerbread trim and picket fences line the narrow red-brick paved paths, which are reserved for the use of spookily silent golf buggies.

JACKSONVILLE ✪✪✪

Founded on the St Johns River in 1822, and named for General Andrew Jackson, the first governor of Florida, Jacksonville is the huge and high-rise capital of the First Coast. This was the original tourist gateway to Florida, though today's visitors tend to head for the Jacksonville Beaches, 12 miles east of downtown, and visit the city's several attractions on day trips.

The heart of the city spans a bend in the river, with the business district and Jacksonville Landing shopping and restaurant complex on the north bank. It is linked to the 1¼-mile Riverwalk along the south bank by a water taxi service, which is a convenient route to the **Museum of Science and History**. This is the place to get to grips with the natural history of the state in a series of well-constructed dioramas, to learn about the ancient Timucua Indians who greeted the first colonial settlers, and to discover more about recent historical events from the Civil War and 1870s steamboat era.

➕ 29E5
🍴 Cafés/restaurants (£–£££)
❓ Jacksonville Jazz Festival, Oct/Nov

Museum of Science and History
✉ 1025 Museum Circle
☎ 904/396 7062
🕐 Mon–Fri 10–5, Sat 10–6, Sun 1–6
♿ Very good
💲 Moderate

The sparkling Jacksonville city skyline

INDEPENDENT LIFE

The Buccaneer Trail

Fernandina's harbour shelters a fleet of shrimping boats

The Buccaneer Trail follows the A1A coast road from the Jacksonville Beaches north to Fernandina Beach. The start point for this drive is the Mayport Ferry, which makes the short journey across the St Johns River to Fort George Island every 30 minutes from 6:15AM to 10:15PM.

On reaching Fort George Island, turn right on the A1A. After 3 miles turn left and continue to the Kingsley Plantation.

Dating from 1798, Florida's oldest plantation home was bought by Zephaniah Kingsley in 1814. The plantation grew Sea Island cotton, sugar cane, citrus and corn, and was worked by around 60 slaves. A neat row of 23 former slave quarters has survived in a clearing in the woods.

Turn left back on to A1A, and head north to the entrance to Little Talbot State Park.

This quiet natural preserve offers a choice of marsh and coastal hammock walks, and 5 miles of unspoilt beach dunes. Keep an eye out for otters and marsh rabbits, and the bird life which is plentiful and varied.

Continue northwards on A1A, which crosses a causeway over the Nassau Sound to reach Amelia Island.

Amelia Island was named after George II's beautiful daughter during a brief period of English rule in 1735. Thirteen miles long and only 2½ miles wide at its broadest point, the island's lovely beaches, and the pretty town of Fernandina Beach (► 76), make it one of Florida's most appealing low-key and relaxed holiday spots.

The quickest route back to the Jacksonville Beaches is to retrace your route down A1A south. Alternatively, take A1A west to join I-95 south for Jacksonville.

Distance
25 miles

Time
Allow a full day with stops

Start point
Mayport
➕ 29E5

End point
Fernandina Beach
➕ 29E5

Lunch
Main Squeeze Juice Bar (£)
✉ 105 S 3 Street,
Fernandina Beach
☎ 904/277 3003

Decorative and fine art is exhibited in the galleries of the Cummer Museum

The **Cummer Museum of Art and Gardens** is worth the trip into Jacksonville alone. In the attractive Riverside residential district, it contains the finest art collection in the northeast, ranging from medieval and Renaissance European art to 20th-century American works, and from pre-Columbian antiquities to Meissen porcelain. The English and Italian gardens behind the museum face on to the river, shaded by a superb spreading live oak tree.

To the north of the city, **Jacksonville Zoo** has been hugely improved and expanded. Old-style cages have been abandoned in favour of more realistic habitat enclosures, and there are more than 800 animals and birds on show including Florida panthers, lions, elephants, giraffes and apes. A mini-train chugs around the 73-acre site and there are regular animal encounter presentations.

On the banks of the St Johns River, the **Fort Caroline National Memorial** marks the spot where French colonists attempted to establish a toehold in Florida in 1564. Timucua Indians helped the 300-man expeditionary force to build a wooden fort named after the French king, Charles IX, but it was destroyed by the Spanish the following year. Today there is a scaled-down reproduction of the 16th-century fort, and nature trails in the woodlands.

The Jacksonville Beaches stretch for around 25 miles south from Atlantic Beach down to the golfing resorts of Ponte Vedra Beach. The nicest section of oceanfront is in the **Kathryn Abbey Hanna Park**. Here, the beach is backed by dunes and a woodland nature preserve with walking and cycle trails, fishing, and a campground.

Cummer Museum of Art and Gardens
- 829 Riverside Avenue
- 904/356 6857
- Tue, Thu 10–9, Wed, Fri, Sat 10–5, Sun 12–5
- Very good
- Moderate

Jacksonville Zoo
- 8605 Zoo Road (off Heckscher)
- 904/757 4462
- Daily 9–5
- Good
- Moderate

Fort Caroline National Memorial
- 12713 Fort Caroline Road
- 904/641 7155
- Daily 9–5
- Good
- Free

Kathryn Abbey Hanna Park
- 500 Wonderwood Drive
- 904/249 4700
- Daily 8–dusk
- Good
- Cheap

Food & Drink

The first rule of eating out in Florida is make sure you are hungry. From the awesome heights of an all-American breakfast to the mile-high Cuban sandwich at lunch and a slap-up seafood dinner at the end of a busy day's sightseeing, Florida portion control errs well beyond the realms of simple generosity.

Sometimes you just have to eat with your fingers

Florida Specialities

In recent years, some of Florida's finest chefs have been perfecting 'Floribbean' cuisine, a delicious fusion of fresh local produce and more exotic Caribbean flavours with a bit of New American and Asian flair thrown in. Otherwise, there are few typically Floridian dishes on the menu, but nobody should miss out on a chance to sample *real* Key lime pie, which should be yellow not green. Down in the Keys, conch fritters or chowder (a rather chewy seafood stew) are local dishes. Farmed alligator meat is usually served well disguised as deep-fried nuggets, but if it appears on the menu in a good restaurant it is well worth trying, and is not dissimilar to chicken.

In northern Florida there are plenty of opportunities to sample southern-style cooking. Grits (a sloppy cornmeal porridge best served with salt, pepper and butter) is something of an acquired taste, but barbecued meats are delicious, and look out for 'blackened' dishes, which are coated with tangy Cajun-style spices.

Seafood

Fresh seafood is always on the menu

Seafood restaurants abound in Florida. Snapper, grouper, yellowtail and pompano are among the top locally caught fish, and dolphin, also known as mahi-mahi, which is a fish not a performing mammal. In southern Florida, stone crabs are harvested from October to April, and in the Panhandle, prawns (known as 'shrimp'), blue crabs and oysters are local treats.

Cuban Cooking

The Latin American influence is strongest in the southern part of the state, particularly Miami. This is the place to sample a Cuban sandwich served in a long roll packed with cheese, ham and pork, and a strong, sweet *café cubano*, a thimble-sized cup of coffee that more than lives up to its nickname: zoom juice. Favourite restaurant dishes include chicken with rice (*arroz con pollo*) and fried beef (*vaca frita*) served with black beans, rice and fried plantain.

Hearty breakfasts served with a smile are the order of the day at this diner

Budget Bites

It is easy to eat out cheaply and well in Florida. Resort areas generally offer a wide choice of family restaurants and familiar fast food chains. Look out for special deals such as Early Bird menus served before the main evening rush, and all-you-can-eat fixed-price buffets. Larger shopping malls generally offer a food court with a selection of different cafés and take-away operations serving anything from pizza and deli sandwiches to Chinese and Tex-Mex dishes. Good ready-made meals and salads are sold in supermarkets, and buying up cold drinks at supermarket prices can save a small fortune.

A snappy advertisement for the local brew

Drinking

Soft drinks are widely available and holidaymakers should be sure to drink plenty in order to avoid dehydration in the hot Florida sunshine.

The legal drinking age is 21 and identification may be required as proof. Wine and beer are available in supermarkets, but spirits can only be bought in a liquor store.

28B5

🍴 Limited in Marianna; concession in the park

Florida Caverns State Park

✉️ 3345 Caverns Road (off SR167)

☎️ 850/482 9598

🕐 Daily 8–dusk; caves 9–4

💲 Cheap

MARIANNA/FLORIDA CAVERNS STATE PARK ⭐⭐

This state park offers a rare opportunity to explore Florida's limestone foundations through a series of stunning underground caverns. Around 65ft below ground, the caverns are decorated with eerily beautiful stalactites and stalagmites and maintain a cool 61–66°F. Above ground, there are woodland hiking trails and bridle paths, a swimming hole on the Chipola River, and a highly recommended 52-mile canoe trail, which follows the river south to the Apalachicola National Forest.

📍 29D4

🍴 Café (£); restaurant (££)

Marjorie Kinnan Rawlings State Historic Site

✉️ CR325, Cross Creek

☎️ 352/466 3672

🕐 Daily 9–5 for tours

♿ Good

💲 Cheap

MICANOPY ⭐⭐

The picture-perfect village of Micanopy with its old brick stores and Victorian homes dozes in the shade of magnificent live oaks planted in a canopy over Cholokka Boulevard. The store fronts may have been quietly hijacked by antiques and curio dealers and the grand Herlong Mansion transformed into a comfortable B&B, but this is a lovely corner of Old Florida. It is also a good base for a trip to the **Marjorie Kinnan Rawlings State Historic Site**, a fascinating Cracker homestead where the Pulitzer prize-winning writer lived during the 1930s and 1940s.

📍 28A5

🍴 Café (£)

Blackwater River State Park

✉️ Off US90 (15 miles NE of Milton)

☎️ 850/983 5363

🕐 Daily 8–dusk

💲 Cheap

MILTON ⭐⭐⭐

Milton is the launch point for a selection of the finest canoeing trails in the state. Several operators (▶ 110) offer a wide range of options from half-day paddles and inner tube rides to three-day expeditions on the Coldwater and Blackwater rivers and Sweetwater and Juniper creeks. Canoe hire can also be arranged from outposts near **Blackwater River State Park**. Here there are hiking trails in the woodlands and swimming in the gently flowing sand-bottomed river, which has sandy beaches along its banks.

Quiet moorings in St Andrews State Recreation Area

Facing page: the gentle splash of the oars along Blackwater canoe trail

PANAMA CITY BEACH

Chief resort of the 'Redneck Riviera', so called for its enormous popularity with holidaymakers from the neighbouring southern states, Panama City Beach fronts 27 miles of broad white sands with a wall of hotels, motels and condominiums. Strung out along this 'Miracle Strip' are amusement parks and arcades, miniature golf courses, shopping malls and family restaurants. Beachfront concessions offer a host of watersports activities, and there is excellent snorkelling and diving (▶ 110–11).

At the heart of the Strip is the Shipwreck Island Water Park, a popular alternative to the beach. It sits back to back with the bright lights and disco delights of the **Miracle Strip Amusement Park**, a nine-acre evening entertainment complex offering 30 fairground rides, from a giant roller-coaster to swinging gondolas and a ferris wheel, plus candy floss, carousels and sideshows.

Panama City Beach has two animal attractions. **Gulf World** concentrates on the marine life side of things, with dolphin and sea lion shows, a walk-through shark tank and assorted aquariums. The small, but evidently well-tended, **Zoo-World** attraction is home to more than 300 animals including bears, big cats, apes and alligators. More than 15 of the animal species here are on the rare and endangered list. There is also a children's petting zoo.

A welcome escape from the busy main beach, **St Andrews State Recreation Area** offers unspoilt dunes, woodland trails, fine swimming and diving in the shallows. There are regular boat trips out to Shell Island for more lazing around on the beach or gentle shell collecting. Shell Island trips are also available from the Treasure Island and Captain Anderson's marinas.

✚ 28B5
🍴 Cafés/restaurants (£–£££)

Miracle Strip Amusement Park
✉ 12000 Front Beach Road
☎ 850/234 3333
🕐 Daily Jun–Labor Day; Fri, Sat Apr–May
♿ Good
💲 Expensive

Gulf World
✉ 15412 Front Beach Road
☎ 850/234 5271
🕐 Daily from 9
♿ Good
💲 Expensive

ZooWorld
✉ 9008 Front Beach Road
☎ 850/230 1065
🕐 Daily 9–dusk
♿ Good
💲 Moderate

St Andrews State Recreation Area
✉ 4415 Thomas Drive
☎ 850/233 5140
🕐 Daily 8–dusk
♿ Limited
💲 Cheap

85

Towers, verandas and gabled roofs are features of the elegant homes built in Pensacola during the 19th century

 28A5
Cafés/restaurants (£–£££)
Milton (➤ 84)
Fiesta of Five Flags, Jun

Historic Pensacola Village
Visitor Center, 205 E Zaragoza Street
850/595 5985
Mon–Sat 10–4. Closed Mon in winter
 Tours: moderate

Fort Pickens National Park
1400 Fort Pickens Road/SR399
850/934 2635
Daily 8:30–dusk
Good
Moderate per car

The ZOO
5701 Gulf Breeze Parkway
850/932 2229
Daily 9–5 in summer, 9–4 in winter
Good
Moderate

PENSACOLA ✪✪✪

Spanish explorer Tristan de Luna made the first attempt to establish a colony at Pensacola in 1559, but the capital of the western Panhandle has to content itself with the title of second most historic town in Florida after St Augustine. However, Pensacola does claim to be the 'Cradle of Naval Aviation', and it is home to the excellent National Museum of Aviation (➤ 20).

The British laid out the city centre in the 1770s, but most of the buildings in the **Historic Pensacola Village** date from the mid-19th-century timber boom era. A stroll around these tree-shaded streets and squares is a great way to spend half a day or so. There are small museums of local history, industry and commerce, a wealth of Victorian architecture, and tours around the interiors of a handful of restored homes.

Across Pensacola Bay, the seafront resort of Pensacola Beach is well-equipped for families and watersports enthusiasts. On the western tip of the barrier island, **Fort Pickens National Park** offers excellent swimming, hiking and cycle trails, and the massive five-sided early-19th century fort is open to the public.

East of Gulf Breeze **The ZOO** houses an exotic menagerie, including white Bengal tigers and snow leopards. The miniature train rides are fun for children and there is a very good petting area.

ST AUGUSTINE (➤ 22, TOP TEN)

A Walk Around St Augustine

The compact historic heart of St Augustine (➤ 22) is the ideal size to explore on foot. This short walk starts from the 18th-century City Gates at the north end of St George Street.

Lined with historic buildings, shops and restaurants, St George Street is the old city's main thoroughfare. Here the Oldest Wooden Schoolhouse (number 14) dates from around 1788, and the fascinating **Spanish Quarter Museum** (number 33) depicts life in the 18th-century colonial town with the help of reconstructed buildings and a working blacksmith's shop. Peña-Peck House (number 143) was originally built for the Spanish Royal Treasurer in the 1740s, but it has been restored and furnished in mid-19th-century style.

At Plaza de la Constitucion, cut diagonally across to the right and take King Street. Cross Cordova Street.

On the right, Flagler College was once the grand Ponce de Leon Hotel, opened in 1888. Visitors are free to enter the foyer and peek into the elaborate Rotunda dining room.

Return to the Plaza and walk down the south side. Turn right on Aviles Street.

The Spanish Military Hospital (number 3) takes an unsentimental look at 18th-century medical practices.

Detour down Artillery Lane (on the right) for the Oldest Store Museum, or continue down Aviles Street to number 20.

The 1797 Ximenez-Fatio House was turned into a boarding house in the 1830s. It has been cleverly restored and each room is furnished in the appropriate style for a variety of 19th-century lodgers from a military man to a lady invalid.

Continue along Aviles. Turn left on Bridge Street, right on Charlotte Street, and left on St Francis Street for the Oldest House.

Watch the blacksmith at work in St Augustine

Distance
1 mile

Time
4 hours with stops

Start point
City Gates, St George Street
🚏 29E5

End point
Oldest House, St Francis Street
🚏 29E5

Lunch
Florida Cracker Café (£-££)
✉ 81 St George Street
☎ 904/829 0397

Spanish Quarter Museum
✉ 33 St George Street
☎ 904/825 6830
🕐 Sun–Thu 9–6, Fri–Sat 9–7
♿ Moderate

28C5

 Cafés/restaurants (£–£££)

 Walk tour maps from the Visitors Center, New Capitol Building (West Plaza Level)

Old Capitol

 S Monroe Street at Apalachee Parkway

☎ 850/487 1902

🕐 Mon–Fri 9–4:30, Sat 10–4:30, Sun and holidays 12–4:30

♿ Good

✋ Free

Museum of Florida History

✉ 500 S Bronough Street

☎ 850/488 1484

🕐 Mon–Fri 9–4:30, Sat 10–4:30, Sun and hols 12–4:30

♿ Very good

✋ Free

Tallahassee Museum of History and Natural Science

✉ 3945 Museum Drive

☎ 850/575 8684

🕐 Mon–Sat 9–5, Sun 12:30–5

♿ Good

✋ Moderate

A B Maclay State Gardens

✉ 3540 Thomasville Road/US319

☎ 850/487 4556

🕐 Daily 8–dusk

♿ Good

✋ Cheap

Right: the Capitol Complex in the heart of Tallahassee

Facing page: a white heron stalks the reeds in Wakulla Springs State Park

TALLAHASSEE ✪✪

Diplomatically sited midway between the two historic cities of St Augustine and Pensacola, the state capital is a fine old southern town just 14 miles from the Georgia border. Tallahassee radiates from the hilltop Capitol Complex, where the turn-of-the-last-century Old Capitol crouches in the shadow of its towering modern successor. Both are open to visitors, and the **Old Capitol** has a number of interesting historic exhibits.

It is a short stroll to the quiet tree-lined streets of the Park Avenue historic district where 19th-century legislators and merchants built gracious homes. Self-guided walk tour maps are available from the Capitol Complex visitor centre and there are tours of the charming Knott House Museum in a restored 1840s house.

Another downtown attraction is the **Museum of Florida History**. Mastodon bones, historical dioramas, colonial, pioneer and Civil War artefacts illustrate a colourful and informative potted history of the state. However, the museum most likely to appeal to young children is the terrific **Tallahassee Museum of History and Natural Science** out in the woods on the shores of Lake Bradford. Laid out in three main areas, the open-air

site contains Big Bend Farm, where volunteers in pioneer costume work the 1880s farm with its animals and crop gardens. Down by the water, a boardwalk trail leads past enclosures for Florida wildlife including bobcats and black bears. A third section preserves a selection of interesting historic buildings.

A favourite excursion from Tallahassee is a visit to the **A B Maclay State Gardens**, just north of the city. These glorious gardens were founded in the 1930s by Alfred B Maclay, and surround his winter home. Naturally, the gardens look their best in the cooler months from December (when the first camellias bloom) until April. In the grounds there is boating on Lake Hall, woodland nature trails and picnicking facilities.

WAKULLA SPRINGS STATE PARK ✪✪✪

South of Tallahassee, one of the world's biggest fresh-water springs bubbles up from the Florida aquifer into a 4½-acre pool at the centre of the park. Snorkelling, swimming and glass-bottomed boat rides provide a first-hand view of the underwater scenery and the water is so clear it is easy to see the bed of the pool 185ft below. Boat trips on the Wakulla River offer good wildlife-spotting opportunities. Look for alligators, deer, turtles, osprey and a wide variety of wading birds.

🔳 28C5
✉ 1 Springs Drive/SR267 (off US319)
☎ 850/922 3633
🕐 Daily 8–dusk
🍴 Concessions (£) and restaurant (£–££)
♿ Good
🎫 Cheap

WHITE SPRINGS ✪

A small town on the Suwannee River, White Springs' claim to fame is the **Stephen Foster State Folk Culture Center**. Born in Pennsylvania in 1826, Foster never even saw the Suwannee but he did make it famous with *Old Folks at Home* (➤ 73), or *Suwannee River*, which he wrote in southern dialect for a minstrel show in 1851.

In the park, a museum displays dolls' house dioramas depicting several of Foster's other famous songs such as *Oh! Susanna* and *Jeanie With The Light Brown Hair*, there are daily carillon recitals, craft shops and pontoon boat rides on a pretty forest-lined stretch of the Suwannee.

🔳 29D5
✉ US41 N (3 miles E of I-95)
☎ 904/397 2733
🕐 Daily 8–dusk; museum 9–5
🍴 Café (£)
♿ Good
🎫 Cheap

Following page: *sailing into the sunset, just off Key West*

Where To...

Above: *colourful neon signs are designed to catch the eye*
Right: *Dixieland jazz at Rosie O'Grady's*

Miami

Prices

Prices are approximate, based on a three-course meal for one without drinks and service:

£ = under $10
££ = $10–$25
£££ = over $25

A Warning

Many restaurants in Miami and other major cities have started to add an automatic service charge of around 15 per cent to the bill. Check whether you have already been charged before counting out the tip.

Arnie and Richie's (£)

A local institution constructing deli sandwiches to die for, piled high with pastrami, cheese, rare roast beef and other mouthwatering delicacies.
✉ 525 41st Street, North Miami Beach ☎ 305/531 7691
🕒 Breakfast, lunch, dinner

Astor Place Bar & Grill (£££)

Amazing atrium setting for sophisticated fusion cuisine with Caribbean/Mediterranean influences such as pumpkin seed-crusted rack of lamb with mint salsa. The fried banana splits are famous.
✉ 956 Washington Avenue, Miami Beach ☎ 305/672 7217
🕒 Lunch, dinner

Balans (£–££)

Terrific value for fashionable Lincoln Road Mall. Wide-ranging Mediterranean/Asian menu plus naughty-but-nice English desserts such as sticky toffee pudding. Outdoor seating offers an alternative to the ever-crowded interior.
✉ 1022 Lincoln Road, Miami Beach ☎ 305/534 9191
🕒 Breakfast, lunch, dinner

Bangkok Bangkok (££)

There are lots of tasty nibbles on the appetizer menu at this popular haunt. Main dishes include spicy Thai curries, noodles and interesting fish dishes.
✉ 157 Giralda Avenue, Coral Gables ☎ 305/444 2397
🕒 Lunch, dinner

Bayside Hut (£)

Hang out with the windsurfing crowd and barefoot yachties at this laidback seafood shack and bar on the water. Check out the catch of the day (snapper and grouper are standards) and don't miss out on the seasoned French fries.
✉ 3501 Rickenbacker Causeway, Key Biscayne ☎ 305/361 0808 🕒 Lunch, dinner

Café Prima Pasta (££)

Be prepared to wait for a table at this excellent pasta place. All the classic dishes benefit from being made with the freshest home-made pastas and sauces.
✉ 414 71st Street, North Miami Beach ☎ 305/867 0106
🕒 Lunch, dinner

Café Tu Tu Tango (££)

World food, from Mediterranean salads and kebabs to designer pizzas and Tex-Mex standards, dished up in a funky artist's loft setting.
✉ CocoWalk, 3015 Grand Avenue, Coconut Grove
☎ 305/529 2222 🕒 Lunch, dinner

Da Leo Trattoria (££)

This popular Italian restaurant spills out on to the Lincoln Road Mall and makes a good lunch stop as well as an evening venue.
✉ 819 Lincoln Road, Miami Beach ☎ 305/674 0350
🕒 Lunch, dinner

Hard Rock Café (££)

No surprises from the rock restaurant chain, but they still pack in the crowds for all the usual burgers, salads and BLTs, with a side order of rock memorabilia.
✉ Bayside Marketplace, 401 Biscayne Boulevard
☎ 305/377 3110 🕒 Lunch, dinner until late

Larios on the Beach (££)

Cuban disco diva Gloria Estefan's great value Ocean Drive eatery offers an alternative to Little Havana. Cuban sandwiches, beef dishes, black beans and seafood paella for two are all worth investigating.

✉ 820 Ocean Drive, Miami Beach ☎ 305/532 9577
🕐 Breakfast, lunch, dinner

Monty's Stone Crab Seafood House & Raw Bar (£££)

Fabulous position on Dinner Key (where old time Coconut Grovers used to picnic) with a huge terrace overlooking Biscayne Bay and a positively dazzling array of seafood specialities including the namesake stone crabs.

✉ 2550 S Bayshore Drive, Coconut Grove ☎ 305/858 1431
🕐 Lunch, dinner

News Café (£)

An Ocean Drive landmark facing the beach. Outdoor tables for prime people-watching and a leisurely brunch. Menu favourites include omelettes, salads, and pasta. Also at 2901 Florida Avenue, Coconut Grove (☎ 305/774 6397).

✉ 800 Ocean Drive, Miami Beach ☎ 305/538 6397
🕐 24 hours

Oasis Café (£)

A vegetarian-friendly eatery, though meat is also served. Treat the tastebuds to Mediterranean-style humous and falafel, and there are huge salads, tofu dishes and seafood on the varied menu.

✉ 976 41st Street, North Miami Beach ☎ 305/674 7676
🕐 Lunch, dinner

Orlando Seafood Restaurant & Fish Market (£)

Be prepared to enjoy your seafood on the hoof, as the Orlando is a stand-up affair. However, this minor inconvenience is reflected in the bargain prices for mouth-watering fish sandwiches and other treats.

✉ 501 NW 37th Avenue ☎ 305/642 6767 🕐 Lunch, dinner

Picnics at Allen's Drug Store (£)

It is Nostalgia City at this old-fashioned all-American diner complete with a jukebox and ice-cream sodas. As befits such surroundings, the best bets are the home-cooked chilli, deli sandwiches, burgers and Key lime pie.

✉ 4000 Red Road, Coral Gables ☎ 305/665 6964
🕐 Breakfast, lunch, dinner

Restaurant St Michel (£££)

Excellent standards of service and an elegant dining room set the scene for the superb, French-influenced New American cuisine.

✉ 162 Alcazar Avenue, Coral Gables ☎ 305/446 6572
🕐 Breakfast, lunch, dinner

Versailles (££)

A legend in its own lifetime, this Little Havana institution is a sort of living slice of Latin American soap opera with food, serving up a massive menu of Cuban goodies to crowds of awestruck tourists and partying Cubanos dressed up to the nines. Good fun and open until late.

✉ 3555 SW 8th Street, Little Havana ☎ 305/444 0240
🕐 Lunch, dinner

The Cuban Cocktail

If you are dining out Cuban-style, go all Old Havana-colonial and order a round of *mojitos*. Made with white rum, lime juice and a sprig of fresh mint, they are absolutely delicious and very refreshing. As well as wine and beer, most Cuban restaurants will also serve chilled *sangria*.

Southern Florida & the Florida Keys

Eating Hours
As a general rule, Florida's restaurants do not stay open late, particularly outside the major cities. Breakfast starts early – around 7; lunch lasts from around noon to 2:30; while dinner can start as early as 5:30 and be wrapped up by 9, though most resort area restaurants will serve until 10:30. Sunday brunch tends to run around 10–2.

Boca Raton
Flakowitz Bagel Inn (£)
This budget lunch stop is bagel heaven, where the Jewish deli roll is transformed into a well-filled work of art. Choose from a selection of meats, cheeses and salads and either eat in or take-out.
- ✉ **19999 N Federal Highway** ☎ **561/368 0666** 🕒 **Breakfast, lunch**

Mark's at the Park (££–£££)
Mark Militello is one of South Florida's most creative and successful chefs and this is an excellent opportunity to sample his stylish Floribbean/ Mediterranean cooking. Cost-conscious diners should check out the pastas and pizzas.
- ✉ **344 Plaza Real, Mizner Park** ☎ **561/395 0770** 🕒 **Lunch, dinner**

Fort Lauderdale
Las Olas Café (££)
Tucked away off Fort Lauderdale's attractive main shopping street, Las Olas Café's garden courtyard is perfect for summer evening meals. The fresh and tasty Floribbean menu offers plenty of choice to tempt adventurous diners.
- ✉ **922 E Las Olas Boulevard** ☎ **954/524 4300** 🕒 **Dinner**

Fort Myers
The Veranda (££)
Housed in a pretty turn-of-the-19th-century historic home, the Veranda also offers balmy courtyard dining in the summer months. The award-winning regional menu features fresh local produce.
- ✉ **2122 2nd Street** ☎ **941/332 2065** 🕒 **Lunch (except Sat), dinner. Closed Sun**

Islamorada
Atlantic's Edge (£££)
A terrific gourmet seafood restaurant in the Cheeca Lodge hotel. Sample the likes of lobster fritters with Key lime aioli, and onion-crusted yellow-tail snapper.
- ✉ **Mile Marker 82** ☎ **305/664 4651** 🕒 **Lunch, dinner**

Green Turtle Inn (££)
This is a great place to sample authentic Keys cuisine from alligator steaks and conch chowder to yellow Key lime pie.
- ✉ **Mile Marker 81.5** ☎ **305/664 9031** 🕒 **Lunch, dinner. Closed Mon**

Key Largo
Mrs Mac's Kitchen (£)
Join the locals at this landmark no-frills diner and bar for the home-cooked all-American breakfasts, fresh seafood and generous daily specials. The dessert pies are a speciality.
- ✉ **Mile Marker 99.4** ☎ **305/451 3722** 🕒 **Breakfast, lunch, dinner. Closed Sun**

Key West
Café Marquesa (£££)
Chef Susan Ferry's award-winning 'Food of the Americas' combines Cajun, Creole and Caribbean influences to effect in this chic but casual haunt.
- ✉ **600 Fleming Street** ☎ **305/292 1919** 🕒 **Dinner**

Pepe's (£)
Friendly local café-diner with outdoor tables in a tree-shaded garden. Hearty breakfasts, seafood, steaks and barbecue.
- ✉ **806 Caroline Street** ☎ **305/294 7192** 🕒 **Breakfast, lunch, dinner**

Rick's Blue Heaven (££)

The motto is 'No shoes, no shirt, no problem' at this laidback spot with trestle tables in the yard and a bathtub full of chilled beer on the bar. Generous helpings of Caribbean barbecue shrimp, chicken jerk and grilled vegetable roulade.

✉ 729 Thomas Street
☎ 305/296 8666 🕐 Lunch, dinner

Naples

Old Naples Pub (£–££)

Cosy wood-panelled pub with a horseshoe bar and old newspaper cuttings adorning the walls. Menu staples include tuna steak salad, fried clams, nachos and grilled chicken sandwiches.

✉ 255 13th Avenue S
☎ 941/649 8200 🕐 Lunch, dinner

Terra (££–£££)

Attractive Mediterranean grill restaurant opening on to the sidewalk. There are interesting salads, focaccia-based pizzas and sandwiches at lunch; pasta, seafood and *osso bucco* at dinner.

✉ 1300 3rd Street S
☎ 941/262 5500 🕐 Lunch, dinner

Palm Beach

Coral Lynn Café (£)

This courtyard café off Worth Avenue is ideal for budget snacks and light meals of salad, sandwiches, fruit shakes and ice-cream.

✉ Via de Lela, 240 Worth Avenue ☎ 561/651 7888
🕐 Lunch

Leopard Lounge and Supper Club (£££)

Leopard skin spots feature in the theatrical décor of this elegant supper club. Enjoy a tempting and varied continental menu, excellent service and nightly entertainment.

✉ The Chesterfield Hotel, 363 Coconut Row ☎ 561/659 5800
🕐 Lunch, dinner

Sanibel and Captiva Islands

Lazy Flamingo II (££)

A casual local spot with a nautical theme and the biggest bar on the island. There is seafood and a raw bar, plus burgers, prime rib sandwiches and Caesar salad with grilled chicken.

✉ 1036 Periwinkle Way, Sanibel ☎ 941/472 6939
🕐 Lunch, dinner

Lighthouse Café (£)

Voted 'Best Breakfast in Lee County'. Deli specials at lunch, and a full evening menu featuring seafood, pasta and other home-cooked dishes in winter time.

✉ 362 Periwinkle Way, Sanibel ☎ 941/472 0303
🕐 Breakfast, lunch; dinner Dec–Easter.

West Palm Beach

It's in the Bag (£)

Great lunch stop and place to watch the world go by in the Clematis Street shopping district. Generously overloaded sandwiches, plus fresh juices and smoothies.

✉ 423 Clematis Street
☎ 561/655 4505 🕐 Lunch

Waterway Café (£–££)

Casual and lively waterfront spot. Seafood, steaks, pasta and pizza.

✉ PGA Boulevard at the Intracoastal, Palm Beach Gardens
☎ 561/694 1700 🕐 Lunch, dinner

Vegetarians

Vegetarians will not find dining out easy in Florida. It is simple to get by without red meat as most menus feature at least a few seafood dishes. But if you do not eat fish the choice tends to be very limited, leaving pasta, pizza and salads (which tend to be pretty dire in budget restaurants).

Central Florida

Eating Out in the Theme Parks

All central Florida's major theme parks offer a variety of dining arrangements. Within SeaWorld, Universal Orlando, Busch Gardens and the Walt Disney World parks the choice ranges from fast food concessions selling hamburgers, hot dogs, ice-creams and cold drinks, to sandwich shops, cafés and full-service restaurants. Reservations for the restaurants are advised and should be made at Guest Relations on entering the park.

Clearwater Beach
Seafood & Sunsets at Julie's (£)

Relaxed and friendly café-restaurant on two floors with outdoor seating. Cuban sandwiches, seafood platters, steaks, salads and killer caramel-nut Turtle Pie dessert.

✉ 351 S Gulfview Boulevard
☎ 727/441 2548 Lunch, dinner

Cocoa Beach
Black Tulip (££)

Cosy, fine dining restaurant in historic Cocoa Village. A Mediterranean influence can be detected in the pasta dishes or tuck into steak au poivre. Lunchtime options include soup and salads.

✉ 207 Brevard Avenue, Cocoa Village ☎ 321/631 1133
 Lunch, dinner

Kissimmee
Pacino's (££)

A welcoming and well-priced family-owned trattoria, which specialises in classic pasta dishes, as well as chargrilled chicken, seafood and meats, served up with a side order of Italian operetta.

✉ 5795 W US192 ☎ 407/239 4141 Dinner

Ponderosa Steakhouse (£)

Family restaurant chain serving a very good value all-you-can-eat buffet laden with steak, chicken, seafood, bread and salads.

✉ 5771 W Irlo Bronson Memorial Highway/US192
☎ 407/397 2100 Breakfast, lunch, dinner

Orlando
Jungle Jim's at Church Street (£)

A useful downtown find for families on a budget – and children love the wildlife décor. Has won awards for 'Orlando's Best Burgers' and 'Best Place for Kids'.

✉ 55 W Church Street
☎ 407/872 3111 Lunch, dinner

Race Rock (££)

Striking motor racing-themed décor, complete with whole cars, bikes and giant trucks, plus pumping rock music and a mile-long menu featuring burgers, pizzas, pasta, Tex-Mex and more.

✉ 8986 International Drive
☎ 407/248 9876 Lunch, dinner

Wolfgang Puck Café (££–£££)

Celebrity chef Wolfgang Puck's California fusion cuisine (that's Mediterranean/Asian influences to the uninitiated) translates perfectly to Florida. Interesting and delicious pizzas, noodles, salads and more.

✉ Downtown Disney Westside, 1482 E Buena Vista Drive ☎ 407/827 7171
 Breakfast, lunch, dinner

St Petersburg Beach
Sea Critters Café (£–££)

Casual dockside dining on the waterfront deck or indoors, and a long and tasty menu including hot fish sandwiches, seafood pasta, spicy Cajun blackened chicken salad and Jamaican jerk.

✉ 2007 Pass-a-Grille Way
☎ 813/360 3706 Lunch, dinner

Ted Peters Famous Smoked Fish (£–££)

Super-casual local spot popular with famished yachties after a day out on the Gulf. Smoked salmon, mackerel and mullet, cold beers and picnic tables.

✉ 1350 Pasadena Avenue, South Pasadena ☎ 727/381 7931 🕐 Lunch, dinner

Sarasota
Chef Caldwell's (£££)
An eclectic but delicious choice of New American, Floribbean and Mediterranean ideas such as tomato-based conch chowder, Maryland crab cakes, rack of lamb, and vegetarian pasta.

✉ 20 S Adams Drive (off St Armands Circle) ☎ 941/388 5400 🕐 Lunch, dinner

Gulf Drive Café (£–££)
Cheap and cheerful casual dining on the waterfront. This is the best kind of breakfast-served-any-time café. As well as omelettes, sandwiches and burgers, there are more substantial evening meals.

✉ 900 Gulf Drive, Bradenton Beach ☎ 941/778 1919 🕐 Breakfast, lunch, dinner

Tampa
Bern's Steak House (£££)
Seriously juicy prime steaks and fresh organic vegetables are the trademark of this famously comfortable and clubby local legend. Reservations are advisable.

✉ 1208 S Howard Avenue ☎ 813/251 2421 🕐 Dinner

Café Creole (££)
An historic tavern with outdoor café tables beneath a red brick arcade, a large bar and a Cajun/Creole influenced menu. Lively atmosphere.

✉ 1330 E 9th Avenue, Ybor City ☎ 813/247 6283 🕐 Lunch, dinner

Walt Disney World Resort
Chef Mickey's (££)
Favourite Disney characters host Chef Mickey's generous buffets. Dinner starts early enough to accommodate the very young. For further information on character dining locations, (► panel).

✉ Disney's Contemporary Resort, 4600 N World Drive ☎ 407/939 3463 🕐 Breakfast, dinner

Hoop-Dee-Doo Musical Revue (£££)
This country-style hoe-down and all-you-can-eat barbecue is one of the most popular Disney dining experiences (► panel).

✉ Disney's Fort Wilderness Resort, 4510 N Fort Wilderness Trail ☎ 407/939 3462 🕐 Dinner

'Ohana (££–£££)
Shape up for a Polynesian-style *luau* feast in Disney's South Seas-themed resort. The hot meats and vegetables are cooked in a traditional-style *imu* barbecue pit, and the portions are gargantuan (► panel).

✉ Disney's Polynesian Resort, 1600 Seven Seas Drive ☎ 407/939 3462 🕐 Dinner

Rainforest Café (££–£££)
An amusement park attraction in its own right, this jungle-themed restaurant in a mini volcano provides its own micro-climate and wildlife as well as an American menu with a Caribbean twist (► panel).

✉ Downtown Disney (Village Marketplace), 1800 E Buena Vista Drive ☎ 407/933 2800 🕐 Lunch, dinner

Disney Character Dining
Even the pickiest child eaters tend to toe the line when promised a dinner date with Mickey Mouse. Disney character dining opportunities kick off at breakfast time when Minnie Mouse appears at the 'Ohana in Disney's Polynesian Resort, and Admiral Goofy and his crew host the Cape May breakfast buffet at the Disney Beach Club Resort. Throughout the day, there are character appearances in the theme park restaurants, too. For current schedules and reservations ☎ 407/939 3463.

Northern Florida

Oystering in Apalachicola

Around 90 per cent of Florida's oyster catch is harvested in Apalachicola Bay. Local oystermen are known as 'tongers' for the scissor-like long-handled tools they use to prise their catch from the oyster beds in the sheltered bay. Oysters can be gathered throughout the year, but must reach a minimum length of 3in before they can be sent to market.

Apalachicola
Apalachicola Seafood Grill and Steakhouse (£–££)
Sample the best of local seafood from oyster stew to smoked oysters, whopper fish sandwiches to the all-you-can-eat fried fish basket.
✉ 100 Market Street
☎ 850/653 9510 🕓 Lunch, dinner

Cedar Key
Blue Desert Café (£)
Kitsch southwestern décor in an old shotgun cottage just east of town, and a long and varied menu of delicious sandwiches, pizzas, pasta and knock-out dessert pies.
✉ 12518 SR24 ☎ 352/543 9111 🕓 Dinner until late. Closed Sun–Mon

Island Hotel (££)
This historic inn specialises in fresh seafood straight off the docks; local treats include blue crabs and clams. Check out the murals in the bar.
✉ 2nd and B Streets
☎ 352/543 5111 🕓 Lunch, dinner. Closed Tue

Daytona
Aunt Catfish's (£–££)
Tasty and amazing value Southern-style cooking plus a great location on the Halifax River. Spit roast chicken, fried shrimp, catfish and crab cakes with hush puppies and a salad bar.
✉ 4009 Halifax Drive, Port Orange ☎ 904/767 4768
🕓 Lunch, dinner

Fernandina Beach
Beech Street Grill (£££)
A nest of attractive modern dining rooms laid out in a lovely old property in Fernandina's historic district. Innovative New American cooking with local seafood, and a notable wine list.
✉ 801 Beech Street
☎ 904/277 3662 🕓 Dinner

Florida House Inn (£)
All-you-can-eat boarding house dinners served up in Florida's oldest hotel. Trestle tables are loaded with platters and bowls of home-cooked southern food.
✉ 20–2 S 3rd Street
☎ 904/261 3300 🕓 Dinner

Fort Walton
Harpoon Hanna's (£)
Beachfront family restaurant and saloon offering a range of seafood dishes and burgers. Live music is provided and there is a big deck for watching the sun go down.
✉ 1450 Miracle Strip Parkway
☎ 850/243 5501 🕓 Lunch, dinner

Gainesville
Panache at the Wine and Cheese Gallery (£)
This deli café makes an ideal lunch stop with outdoor patio tables for fine weather. Choose from a good selection of home-made soups and salads, sandwiches and fine cheeses.
✉ 113 N Main Street
☎ 352/372 8446 🕓 Lunch, dinner

Jacksonville
Dolphin Depot (££)
Very popular and very good seafood restaurant noted for its excellent daily specials. The Depot dolphin fish with matchstick sweet potatoes and home-made chutney is a house speciality.
✉ 704 N 1st Street, Jacksonville Beach ☎ 904/270 1424 🕓 Dinner

Southend Brewery & Smokehouse (££)

A water's edge restaurant with a micro-brewery at its heart and the tantalising aroma of the smokehouse. Hearty racks of ribs, ale-steamed sausages and bbq dishes, rich pies and brownies, plus specialty beers.

✉ Jacksonville Landing
☎ 904/665 0000 🕔 Lunch, dinner

Panama City Beach
Capt Anderson's (££–£££)

Great harbourfront location for one of the best restaurants in town. Seafood heads up the menu, and the Greek salads are a speciality.

✉ 5551 N Lagoon Drive
☎ 850/234 2225 🕔 Dinner

Pensacola
Chan's Gulfside (£–££)

Take your pick from the casual café downstairs serving good sandwiches and light meals; or the upstairs dining room, which specialises in delicious and innovative Floribbean seafood dishes.

✉ 2½ Via De Luna, Pensacola Beach ☎ 850/932 3525
🕔 Lunch, dinner

Jaime's (£££)

Lovely historic home, with an art deco interior and classy wide-ranging menu drawing on Floribbean and continental influences.

✉ 424 E Zaragoza Street
☎ 850/434 2911 🕔 Dinner. Closed Sun

McGuire's Irish Pub (£)

A rollicking Irish-American pub with a good atmosphere, a busy bar and home-brewed beers. Diners will find ribs, burgers, seafood and other pub grub favourites on the menu.

✉ 600 E Gregory Street
☎ 850/433 6789 🕔 Lunch, dinner

St Augustine
Cap's Seafood (£–££)

A friendly and unpretentious local bar and restaurant on the water with a rustic, woodsy interior. Excellent seafood served Southern style and Florida specials such as gator tail.

✉ 4325 Myrtle Road, North Beach ☎ 904/824 8794
🕔 Lunch, dinner

Raintree (£££)

Lovely setting in a restored historic building, friendly service, and a well-balanced seasonal menu that includes plenty of fresh seafood and notable home-made desserts.

✉ 102 San Marco Avenue
☎ 904/824 7211 🕔 Dinner

Tallahassee
Andrew's Capital Grill and Bar (£–££)

New York-style deli and grill in the restored downtown district with outdoor seating. Upstairs, Andrew's Second Act is one of the best restaurants in town (£££).

✉ 228 S Adams Street
☎ 850/222 3444 🕔 Lunch, dinner

Po'Boys Creole Café (£)

Check into Po'Boys to sample the enormous namesake po'boy sandwiches. Creole specialities, cold beers and New Orleans inspired atmosphere and entertainment.

✉ 224 E College Avenue
☎ 850/224 5400 🕔 Lunch, early dinner

Dining with Children

Families travelling with young children can breathe a sigh of relief when they arrive in Florida. The states' child-friendly attitude extends to restaurants of all descriptions. Staff will usually make great efforts to see that children are welcomed and children's menus are widely available; if you do not see one on display, always ask.

Miami

Avalon/Majestic (££)

Two classic art deco hotels with modern amenities facing the beach at the heart of the SoBe scene. Both hotels have restaurants and lounges and the staff are friendly and helpful.

⊠ **700 Ocean Drive, Miami Beach** ☎ **305/538 0133 or 1-800 933 3306**

Banana Bungalow (£)

Funky hotel designed for the young and hip on a budget. There are 60 dormitories and rooms a block from the beach and within walking distance of Ocean Drive. Pool and bar.

⊠ **2360 Collins Avenue, Miami Beach** ☎ **305/538 1951 or 1-800 746 7835**

Biltmore Hotel (£££)

Luxurious 1920s Mediterranean Revival-style landmark with grand public rooms and spacious accommodation. There is an excellent restaurant; a magnificent outdoor pool, tennis, and golf.

⊠ **1200 Anastasia Avenue, Coral Gables** ☎ **305/445 1926 or 1-800 727 1926**

Brigham Gardens (££)

Enchanting small guesthouse set in tropical gardens close to the beach and Lincoln Road Mall. Eighteen well-equipped rooms, studios and one-bed apartments in either an art deco or a Mediterranean-style building.

⊠ **1411 Collins Avenue, Miami Beach** ☎ **305/531 1331**

Clay Hotel and International Hostel (£)

This hotel has 106 beds in dormitories and rooms housed in a lovely old Spanish-style building right at the heart of SoBe on central Espanola Way. Bar and gardens. Book ahead.

⊠ **1438 Washington Avenue, Miami Beach** ☎ **305/534 2988 or 1-800 379 CLAY**

Delano Hotel (£££)

One of Miami's coolest hotels strikes a pose on the oceanfront. The décor is minimalist chic, the atmosphere superior, and the restaurant very good. Facilities include a pool and fitness centre.

⊠ **1685 Collins Avenue, Miami Beach** ☎ **305/672 2000 or 1-800 555 5001**

The Governor (£–££)

There are 125 attractive rooms in this lovely art deco building on a quiet side street a block from the ocean and close to Lincoln Road Mall. Restaurant, garden and pool.

⊠ **435 21st Street, Miami Beach** ☎ **305/532 2100 or 1-800 542 0444**

Hampton Inn (££)

This mainland hotel provides a convenient base for sightseeing, shopping and dining in the Grove. There is a pool and the tariff is inclusive of breakfast.

⊠ **2800 SW 28th Terrace, Coconut Grove** ☎ **305/448 2800**

Wyndham Miami Beach Resort (£££)

This huge, refurbished hotel is right on the oceanfront and offers excellent watersports facilities. It is particularly good for families with children.

⊠ **4833 Collins Avenue, Miami Beach** ☎ **305/532 3600 or 1-800 221 8844**

Southern Florida & the Florida Keys

Fort Lauderdale

Sea Chateau (£)

Attractive small property with 17 rooms and spacious self-catering accommodation a short walk from the beach. Pool; complimentary breakfast; children under 12 free.

✉ 555 N Birch Road
☎ 954/566 8331 or 1-800 726 3732

Fort Myers

Best Western Pink Shell Beach Resort (££–£££)

Beachfront family resort with a choice of hotel rooms, condos and cottages. Facilities include pool, tennis and watersports.

✉ 275 Estero Boulevard, Fort Myers Beach ☎ 941/463 6181 or 1-800 449 1830

Islamorada

Cheeca Lodge (£££)

Quiet, low-rise resort complex on the oceanside. Excellent fishing and diving, children's programmes, and gourmet dining.

✉ Mile Marker 82.5
☎ 305/664 4651 or 1-800 327 2888

Key Largo

Holiday Inn Sunspree Resort & Marina (££–£££)

Comfortable, well-equipped rooms in a huge resort ideally suited for a family holiday. Swimming pools, watersports and boating facilities, activity programmes, and dining.

✉ Mile Marker 100
☎ 305/451 2121 or 1-800 843 5397

Key West

Southernmost Motel (££)

Attractive and popular hotel base within walking distance of the town centre.

Tropical décor brightens up the large and comfortable rooms, and palms flank the pool areas.

✉ 1319 Duval Street
☎ 305/296 6577 or 1-800 354 4455

Wicker Guesthouse (££)

A conveniently central and cosy B&B guesthouse with pretty rooms and studios. Relax in the secluded gardens and whirlpool.

✉ 913 Duval Street
☎ 305/296 4275 or 1-800 880 4275

Naples

Olde Naples Inn & Suites (££)

Bright, spacious and thoughtfully equipped rooms close to the beach and Third Street South shops and restaurants.

✉ 801 3rd Street S
☎ 941/262 5194 or 1-800 637 6036

Palm Beach

Palm Beach Historic Inn (££)

Charming and surprisingly affordable Victorian-style B&B at the heart of town and a short walk from the beach. The romantic rooms are furnished with antiques.

✉ 365 S County Road
☎ 561/832 4009

Sanibel and Captiva Islands

South Seas Plantation (£££)

Large, attractively landscaped resort with hotel rooms, condos and cottages, beach, pools, marina and a host of family and sporting activities.

✉ 5400 Plantation Road, Captiva ☎ 941/472 5111 or 1-800 449 1827

Seasonal Variations

Room prices can vary dramatically from season to season in Florida. In central and southern Florida, and the Florida Keys, the high season is December to April. During summer room rates can drop by as much as 40 per cent, and it is well worth bargaining if you have not paid for your accommodation in advance. In the north, high season rates apply from October to April. It is worth bearing in mind that Florida is a popular family destination and holiday periods can be busy.

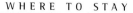

Central Florida

Reservations

Reservations can be made by telephone, fax or mail, and should be made as early as possible in high season (► 101, panel) and holiday periods. A deposit (usually by credit card) equivalent to the nightly rate will ensure your room is held until 6PM; if you are arriving later inform the hotel. Credit card is the preferred payment method in most hotels. Payment by travellers' cheques or cash may have to be made in advance.

Cocoa Beach
Wakulla Motel (££)

Comfortable two-bedroom family holiday apartments with fully equipped kitchens. Set in tropical gardens with pools, sun deck and barbecues close to the beach.

✉ 3550 N A1A ☎ 321/783 2230 or 1-800 992 5852

Kissimmee
Howard Johnson Inn Maingate East (£–££)

Sprawling HoJo property conveniently close to Walt Disney World Resort (free shuttle), shops and restaurants. Large rooms, popular with families, babysitting service, swimming pool, airport bus.

✉ 6051 W Highway 192 ☎ 407/396 1748 or 1-800 288 4678

Orlando
Best Western Plaza International (££)

Large, well-equipped chain hotel with rooms and family suites close to SeaWorld, Walt Disney World Resort and airport bus services; pool. There are good children's facilities and a babysitting service.

✉ 8738 International Drive ☎ 407/345 8195 or 1-800 654 7160

Radisson Hotel Universal (££)

Smart, well-priced hotel close to Universal Studios and I-Drive. Excellent facilities include four restaurants and lounges, a pool, jacuzzi and fitness room, a shopping arcade, and playground.

✉ 5780 Major Boulevard ☎ 407/351 1000 or 1-800 327 2110

St Pete Beach
TradeWinds Sirata Beach Resort (££)

Big beachfront property with spacious rooms, a restaurant, lively tiki bar and pool. Watersports rentals are available.

✉ 5390 Gulf Boulevard ☎ 727/367 2771 or 1-800 344 5999

Sarasota
Helmsley Sandcastle (££–£££)

Family resort overlooking the Gulf of Mexico with spacious rooms, restaurants, a lounge, and pool bar. Sailboat and watersports rentals on site.

✉ 1540 Ben Franklin Drive, Lido Key ☎ 941/388 2181 or 1-800 225 2181

Lido Beach Palms (££)

Comfortable one- and two-bedroom apartments/ efficiencies in a Key West-style complex.

✉ 148 Cleveland Drive, Lido Key ☎ 941/383 9505 or 1-800 237 9505

Walt Disney World Resort
Disney's All-Star Sports and Music Resorts (£–££)

Two good value themed resorts adorned with either sporting or musical motifs.

✉ 1701-1801 W Buena Vista Lake Drive ☎ All-Star Sports. 407/939 5000; All-Star Music, 407/939 6000; reservations, 407/934 7639

Disney's Caribbean Beach Resort (££)

Large, comfortable rooms in five tropically landscaped 'villages', each boasting a pool and lakeside beach.

✉ 900 Cayman Way ☎ 407/934 3400; reservations, 407/934 7639

Northern Florida

Apalachicola

Coombs House Inn (£–££)

Lovely Victorian B&B in a grand old home furnished with antiques (some four-poster beds) and within walking distance of shops and restaurants. Some rooms in a cottage across the street.

✉ 80 6th Street ☎ 850/653 9199

Daytona Beach

Bahama House (££)

Attractive and well laid-out Caribbean-themed efficiencies with ocean views. The hotel is right on the beach and also has a pool. Children's activities are available.

✉ 2001 S Atlantic Avenue, Daytona Beach Shores ☎ 904/248 2001 or 1-800 571 2001

Fernandina Beach

Amelia Island Plantation (£££)

A superb resort property set in 1,000 acres of woodland, beach dunes and golf courses. Lavishly equipped and attractive hotel rooms, condos and villas, fine dining and matchless facilities.

✉ 3000 First Coast Highway ☎ 904/261 6161 or 1-800 874 6878

Florida House Inn (££)

Lovingly restored historic B&B inn with 11 rooms, a restaurant (▶ 98), and a garden in the centre of town. In the evening, the friendly bar is a local favourite.

✉ 20–2 S 3rd Street ☎ 904/261 3300

Fort Walton

Leeside Inn & Marina (£)

Rooms and efficiences in a family resort adjoining the Gulf Islands National Seashore on Okaloosa Island. Restaurant; pool; watersports and fishing.

✉ 1350 US98 E ☎ 904/243 7359 or 1-800 8242747

Pensacola Beach

The Dunes (££)

A good family hotel offering spacious, sunny rooms overlooking the Gulf of Mexico. Facilities include a café, bar, pool, tennis, and children's activities; golfing packages available.

✉ 333 Fort Pickens Road ☎ 850/932 3536 or 1-800 833 8637

St Augustine

Bayfront Inn (£–££)

Right on the waterfront, this Spanish-style inn with a pool is also close to the historic district attractions, shops and restaurants

✉ 138 Avenida Menendez ☎ 904/824 1681 or 1-800 558 3455

Casablanca Inn (££)

Pretty B&B accommodation in an attractively restored inn with antique furnishings and bay views. Conveniently close to all the sights and restaurants; bicycles available for exploring further afield.

✉ 24 Avenida Menendez ☎ 904/829 0928 or 1-800 826 2626

Tallahassee

Ramada Inn (£)

Comfortable if plain rooms and complimentary breakfasts in a large chain hotel close to the city centre. There is a restaurant and bar, a pool and fitness facilities.

✉ 2900 N Monroe Street ☎ 850/386 1027 or 1-800 272 6232

Bed and Breakfast

Florida's B&B inns make a lovely change from the big resort hotels. Most B&Bs are in restored historic homes and the rooms are individually furnished with antiques. In some places mod cons such as television have been banished. Breakfasts are usually huge and feature delicious home-cooked breads and pastries, cereals, eggs and bacon, cheeses and fresh fruit. If you are travelling with the family, check ahead, as some places do not accept children under 12.

Shopping Districts & Malls

Souvenir Suggestions
Florida is the capital of kitsch and just the place to pick up flashing flamingo Christmas lights, an alligator-shaped ashtray or a can of Florida sunshine. T-shirt bargains abound, but do check for quality; Western wear, such as cowboy boots, check shirts and belts, is also popular. Sponges and sea shells from the Gulf of Mexico are light and easy to pack. On the food front, citrus candies and jams, Key lime products from the Florida Keys, and hot sauce and barbecue marinades bring home the taste of Florida.

Sales Tax
Though shopping in Florida is generally a bargain for overseas visitors, be prepared for the local sales tax, which is not included in the displayed price. Sales tax varies from county to county, but averages around 6 per cent, and will be added to the bill at the point of sale.

Miami

Bal Harbour Shops
A luxurious collection of European designer boutiques and the top US department stores Neiman Marcus and Saks Fifth Avenue in Miami's most exclusive shopping mall.
✉ **9700 Collins Avenue, Miami Beach** ☎ **305/866 0311**

Bayside Marketplace
(► 32)

CocoWalk
Boutiques, bistros and souvenirs at the heart of the fun Coconut Grove shopping district. More of the same (plus a great bookstore) at The Streets of Mayfair, 2911 Grand Avenue.
✉ **3015 Grand Avenue, Coconut Grove** ☎ **305/444 0777**

Lincoln Road Mall
This funky pedestrian street boasts an entertaining mix-ture of art galleries, boutiques and speciality stores from designer lighting emporiums to hand-rolled cigars. Restaur-ants and sidewalk cafés revive weary shoppers.
✉ **924 Lincoln Road, Miami Beach** ☎ **305/531 3442**

Southern Florida and the Florida Keys

Boca Raton
Royal Palm Plaza
Appropriately clad in pretty pink stucco, this attractive open-air mall harbours around 80 smart little boutiques, jewellers, galleries, beauty salons and cafés.
✉ **N Federal Highway/US1 (south of Palmetto Park Road)** ☎ **561/362 8247**

Fort Lauderdale
Las Olas Boulevard
This attractive downtown shopping street is well stocked with boutiques and galleries. The new Las Olas Riverfront shopping and dining complex overlooks the New River.
✉ **Las Olas Boulevard** ☎ **954/480 4942**

Key West
Duval and Simonton Streets
While Duval is Key West's busiest shopping street, there are a couple of factory stores on Simonton. Check out the tropical prints at Key West Fabrics and Fashions (number 201); and the designs at The T-Shirt Factory (number 316).

Naples
Third Street South and the Avenues
This charming small shopping and dining enclave offers a tempting selection of contemporary fashion and resort wear boutiques, modern art galleries and speciality shops.
✉ **3rd Street S (between Broad and 14th Avenues S)** ☎ **941/649 6707**

Palm Beach
Worth Avenue
Small but perfectly formed, and great for window-shopping, the upscale shopping enclave of Worth Avenue comprises four gracious little blocks lined with a collection of the world's most expensive designer boutiques, art galleries and jewellers.
✉ **Worth Avenue (between S Ocean Boulevard and Coconut Row)** ☎ **561/659 6090**

West Palm Beach

The Gardens Mall

An enormous indoor mall with more than 160 shops and restaurants. The Gardens also contains a food court and five department stores, including Macy's, Bloomingdale's, Sears and Saks Fifth Avenue.

✉ 3101 PGA Boulevard, Palm Beach Gardens ☎ 561/775 7750

Central Florida

Cocoa/Cocoa Beach

Historic Cocoa Village

This quiet little corner of old Cocoa boasts an appealing selection of craft shops, gift stores, boutiques and cafés laid out along brick-paved sidewalks and shady lanes.

✉ Brevard Avenue (S of SR520) ☎ 321/631 9075

Merritt Square Mall

Space Coast shopping and entertainment complex.

✉ 777 E Merritt Island Causeway/SR520 ☎ 321/452 3272

Kissimmee

Old Town Kissimmee

There is all the fun of the fair at this Old West style open-air mall, which offers around 70 souvenir stores, clothing and gift shops, plus dining and fairground amusement rides to entertain children.

✉ 5770 W Irlo Bronson Memorial Highway/US192 ☎ 407/396 4888

Orlando

Church Street Station Exchange

A popular downtown attraction, the attractive Victorian-style Exchange mall provides a good mix of boutiques, souvenirs, gifts and novelty shops, as well as a food court for cheap dining.

✉ Church Street Station (Exchange Building), 129 W Church Street ☎ 407/422 2434

Florida Mall

Central Florida's largest and most popular shopping destination with over 250 shops and restaurants and five department stores including Saks Fifth Avenue. Most of the top US brand-name fashion stores are here and there is a well-stocked Warner Bros Studio Store.

✉ 8001 S Orange Blossom Trail/US441 ☎ 407/851 6255

Park Avenue

The smart Orlando suburb of Winter Park offers a relaxing alternative to the big shopping malls. Browse in the fashionable boutiques, gifts, crafts and art galleries along the avenue.

✉ Park Avenue at New York Avenue ☎ 407/644 8281

St Petersburg

The Pier

More of a sightseeing feature than a major shopping experience, but very popular nonetheless. A variety of small boutiques and stores sell fashion, gifts and souvenirs. There is also dining with waterfront views.

✉ 800 2nd Avenue NE ☎ 727/821 6164

Tyrone Square

The biggest mall in the Tampa Bay area, with over 155 shops anchored by four department stores including Burdines and Sears, plus dining and movies.

✉ 66th Street and 22nd Avenue N ☎ 727/347 5419

The Great Merchandise Heist

If theme park admission were not enough to seriously dent your wallet, dozens of tempting merchandise outlets make it easy to spend a second unscheduled fortune on T-shirts, cuddly toys and other must-have souvenirs. One way to avoid this pitfall is to make a deal with children about what they can expect to take home, and stick to it. Visitors to Walt Disney World can save valuable sightseeing time by shopping at the one-stop World of Disney superstore (▶ 106).

105

Antiques and Collectibles

Several Florida towns boast antiques districts which can be quite fun to explore, though the goods on sale could be described more accurately as bric-à-brac. Genuine Victoriana includes dolls, linens, glass and small furnishings. 'Collectibles' covers everything else, from the contents of the attic and the garden shed to entertaining Florida souvenirs of the 1920s and 30s.

Sarasota
St Armands Circle

Downtown has The Quay mall, but St Armands Circle's collection of up-market boutiques, galleries, speciality stores and cafés is much more tempting.

 St Armands Key (SR789)
☎ **941/388 1554**

Tampa
Old Hyde Park Village

This attractive, tree-shaded shopping village is a pleasant place to browse. It boasts some 60 boutiques, gift and cook shops as well as restaurants and a cinema.

✉ **Swann and Dakota Avenues**
☎ **813/251 3500**

West Shore Plaza

Tampa's top fashion mall offers a wide selection of men's and women's clothing, accessories, children's clothes and an FAO Schwartz toy store, plus three department stores, restaurants and a food court.

✉ **Westshore and Kennedy Boulevards** ☎ **813/286 0790**

Walt Disney World
Downtown Disney Marketplace

Home to a selection of souvenir and gift shops, but most importantly the vast and dangerously tempting World of Disney, the largest Disney merchandise store on the planet.

✉ **Buena Vista Drive, Lake Buena Vista** ☎ **407/828 3058**

Northern Florida

Daytona
Beach Street

The restored historic shopfronts along downtown Beach Street harbour a collection of speciality shops from antique collectibles to the Angell & Phelps Chocolate Factory (tours and free samples).

Jacksonville
Jacksonville Landing

A downtown landmark on the north bank of the St Johns River, the Landing combines around 65 boutiques, gift shops and speciality stores with a food court and several restaurants.

✉ **2 Independent Drive**
☎ **904/353 1188**

Panama City Beach
Panama City Mall

This shopping, dining and entertainment complex has more than 90 shops anchored by three department stores, plus a food court, cinema and family games room.

✉ **SR77 at 23rd Street (off US231), Panama City**
☎ **850/785 9587**

Pensacola
Cordova Mall

Pensacola's premier shopping centre combines more than 140 fashion outlets, speciality shops and restaurants with a selection of department stores including Dillard's, Gayfers, and Montgomery Ward.

✉ **5100 N 9th Avenue at Bayou Boulevard** ☎ **850/477 5563**

Tallahassee
Governor's Square

This popular shopping centre provides a wide selection of fashion, sportswear, books, music and gifts, restaurants, and four department stores conveniently close to downtown.

✉ **1500 Apalachee Parkway**
☎ **850/671 INFO**

Discount Outlets & Bargain Stores

Southern Florida and the Florida Keys

Florida City
Prime Outlets at Florida City

South of Miami, 45 factory outlet stores offering 25–75 per cent off retail prices on Levis, Nike footwear, OshKosh B'Gosh and more. There is also a food court and children's playground.

✉ **250 E Palm Drive (off US1 and Florida Turnpike)**
☎ **305/248 4727**

Fort Lauderdale
Sawgrass Mills

West of the Florida Turnpike, the world's largest discount outlet mall; 300 brand-name and designer stores include Neiman Marcus Last Call and Sak's off Fifth Avenue.

✉ **W Sunrise Boulevard at Flamingo Road, Sunrise**
☎ **954/846 2350**

Fort Myers
Tanger Sanibel Factory Outlet Stores

Just east of the Sanibel Causeway, this mainland outlet mall offers bargain prices on clothing, footwear and accessories.

✉ **20350 Summerlin Road**
☎ **941/454 1974**

Central Florida

Ellenton
Prime Outlets Ellenton

Just south of Tampa Bay, this is one of the largest factory outlet malls on the Gulf coast. More than 135 designer and name-brand stores.

✉ **5461 Factory Shops Boulevard (I-75/Exit 43)**
☎ **941/723 1150 or 1-888 260 7608**

Orlando
Belz Factory Outlet World
(► panel)

✉ **5401 W Oakridge Road**
☎ **407/352 9611**

Lake Buena Vista Factory Stores

Over 30 factory-direct outlet stores close to Walt Disney World Resort. Get 20 to 75 per cent discounts on sportswear, jeans, and more.

✉ **15591 S Apopka-Vineland Road/SR535** ☎ **407/238 9301**

Northern Florida

Daytona
Daytona Flea and Farmer's Market

This sprawling 40-acre spread of booths and stalls, selling anything and everything from clothing to bric-à-brac at bargain prices, is a popular weekend (Fri–Sun) excursion.

✉ **1425 Tomoka Farms Road/US92 (at I-95)** ☎ **904/253 3330**

Panama City
Manufacturers' Outlet Center

A selection of well-known US brand name manufacturers offering fashion, children's clothing, books, cosmetics and household goods at up to 70 per cent off retail prices.

✉ **105 W 23rd Street (W of SR231), Panama City**
☎ **850/763 9847**

St Augustine
St Augustine Outlet Center

Take advantage of discounts ranging from 25 to 75 per cent on a wide selection of fashions, children's clothing, footwear, accessories and toys from 90-plus outlet stores at this extensive mall

✉ **I-95/Exit 95 at SR16**
☎ **904/825 1555**

Bargain Belz

For shopaholics, the vast Belz Factory Shopping World in Orlando exercises all the inexorable pull of a major theme park. There are two full-scale malls and four annexes, containing 170 outlet stores offering a staggering range of discounted clothing, footwear, sporting goods, cosmetics, toys and accessories. And that is not all. Along with the Belz, the top end of International Drive is awash with bargains, from fashions at the International Designer Outlet Mall to Disney Gifts at the Quality Outlet Center.

Water Parks, Zoos & Museums

Travelling with Children

Florida is probably the ultimate child-friendly holiday destination, but a couple of advance preparations can make your trip even more enjoyable – and safer. If you need child seats in your rented car, be sure to book them in advance. Hotels will provide cots, but these also are best reserved ahead. High-factor sunblock is a must for all children and can be purchased at any supermarket or drug store. Sun hats are a good idea, and make sure children get plenty to drink in the heat.

Miami

American Police Hall of Fame

Gory displays on crime and punishment, the chance to play detective and assorted gangster memorabilia appeal particularly to older children.

⊠ 3801 Biscayne Boulevard
☎ 305/573 0070 ⓓ Daily 10–5:30

Miccosukee Indian Village and Airboat Tours

A half-day excursion out towards the northern entrance to the Everglades National Park at Shark Valley (▶ 41). Touristy alligator wrestling and Seminole Indian crafts, but the Everglades airboat rides are fun.

⊠ Tamiami Trail/US41 (30 miles W of downtown)
☎ 305/223 8380 ⓓ Daily 9–5

Southern Florida and the Florida Keys

Fort Lauderdale
Butterfly World

To the west of town, thousands of brightly coloured butterflies flutter about the giant tropical aviaries at this popular attraction. There is also a hummingbird aviary and a museum of bugs and creepy-crawlies.

⊠ 3600 W Sample Road (I-95/Exit 36), Coconut Creek
☎ 954/977 4434 ⓓ Mon–Sat 9–5, Sun 1–5

Marathon
Museum of Natural History of the Florida Keys

An excellent small museum designed with children in mind. Exhibits include a pygmy sperm whale's skull

impaled on a swordfish, Indian canoes, touch tanks and rescued birds of prey.

⊠ Mile Marker 50 ☎ 305/743 9100 ⓓ Mon–Sat 9–5, Sun 12–5

Naples
Teddy Bear Museum

Over 3,000 toy and ornamental bears of all sizes and descriptions inhabit this cutesy museum in the woods. There is bear art, bear dioramas, Saturday morning bear story readings, and the inevitable bear gift shop.

⊠ 2511 Pine Ridge Road
☎ 941/598 2711 ⓓ Wed–Sat 10–5, Sun 1–5. Closed Mon (except Dec–Apr) and Tue

West Palm Beach
Dreher Park Zoo

A very good small zoo with plenty of shade. Highlights include endangered Florida panthers, and children are always delighted by the woolly llamas and lumbering giant tortoises.

⊠ 1301 Summit Boulevard
☎ 561/547 9453 ⓓ Daily 9–5

Central Florida

Kissimmee
Green Meadows Petting Farm

A real treat for little children, who can find the theme parks quite overwhelming. In a shady farmyard setting, they can experience animal encounters with calves, lambs, ducklings and ponies. Picnickers welcome.

⊠ 1368 S Poinciana Boulevard
☎ 407/846 0770 ⓓ Daily 9:30–5:30 (last tour at 4)

Orlando
Wet 'n' Wild

Twenty-five acres of watery

fun at the best water park in the area outside Walt Disney World Resort. Tackle some of the highest and fastest speed slides in the world, or take a gentle tube ride down the Lazy River. Kiddie pools and sunbathing decks.

✉ 6200 International Drive
☎ 407/351 1800 or 1-800 992 9453 🕓 Daily from 9 in summer, 10 in winter. Call for schedules

Space Coast
US Astronaut Hall of Fame
Just along from the Kennedy Space Center (➤ 17), the Hall of Fame offers an exciting and accessible array of space exhibits, 'hands-on' displays, and stomach-churning simulator rides, plus a rather gentler ride in a full-scale mock-up of a space orbiter.

✉ 6225 Vectorspace Boulevard/SR405, Titusville
☎ 321/269 6100 🕓 Daily 9–5

Tampa
Lowry Park Zoo
It is not just the small-scale inhabitants of the Children's Village (including pygmy goats and Vietnamese pot-bellied piglets) that will appeal here. The Manatee and Aquatic Center and the Discovery Centers' Insect Zoo are big favourites.

✉ 7530 North Boulevard
☎ 813/935 8552 🕓 Daily 9:30–5 (extended in summer)

Northern Florida

Jacksonville Beaches
Adventure Landing
A pirate-themed summer season water park is the main attraction here. Children can also let swing in the baseball batting cages,

play miniature golf and race go-karts. On rainy days, there are indoor laser tag and arcade games.

✉ 1944 Beach Boulevard
☎ 904/246 4386 🕓 Daily 10AM–2AM

Panama City Beach
Junior Museum of Bay County
A low-key attraction for younger children, this small museum adopts a 'hands-on' approach to science, art and nature exhibits. There are games in a life-size teepee, and chickens and ducks to feed in a re-created pioneer homestead.

✉ 1731 N Jenks Avenue, Panama City ☎ 850/769 6128
🕓 Tue–Fri 9–4:30, Sat 10–4

Shipwreck Island Water Park
Six acres of watery thrills and spills, lazy inner tube rides and speed slides. Little children are well catered for in the Tadpole Hole play area, and there are sunbathing decks and restaurants.

✉ 12000 Front Beach Road
☎ 850/234 2282 🕓 Jun–Labor Day 10:30–5:30; reduced hours Apr–May and Sep (call for schedules). Closed Oct–Mar

St Augustine
St Augustine Alligator Farm and Zoological Park
When the children have had their fill of history, cross the bay to Anastasia Island and take them to the World's Original Alligator Farm founded in 1893. Twenty-three species of crocodilians, plus bird shows and farm animals in the petting zoo.

✉ 999 Anastasia Boulevard (A1A) ☎ 904/824 3337
🕓 Daily 9–5

Theme Park Survival
The chief rule is don't overdo it. Young children in particular can find the major theme parks overwhelming and it is best to tailor your visit to their energy levels. Rent a stroller so little children can always hitch a ride, and take plenty of short breaks. Make sure young children carry some form of identification, such as a wrist tag, in case they get lost. And be warned: many of the more extreme thrill rides are limited to passengers measuring 44 inches or taller.

Sporting Activities

Ocean Reafforestation

Pollution, careless boaters and divers have taken a heavy toll on areas of Florida's natural coral reef. In addition to strict controls, one way of addressing the problem has been the introduction of artificial reef sites at depths between 15 and 400ft. This deliberate 'ocean reafforestation' programme has been a runaway success, creating healthy aquatic communities with an exciting variety of fish and other marine creatures and even new coral growth, both on the artificial sites and around sections of rejuvenated natural reef.

Canoeing and Kayaking

Florida's rivers and back bays offer a wealth of canoeing opportunities from a couple of hours' gentle paddle in a state park to a backcountry marathon along the 99-mile Wilderness Waterway, which traverses the Everglades between Flamingo and Everglades City. Most state parks with a suitable stretch of river or waterfront have canoes for rent. Private tour and rental operations abound in prime canoeing areas like the Florida Keys, the Gulf islands and the Panhandle. The following is just a short list of top self-guided canoeing trails and tour operators:

Miami

Miami Beach
Urban Trails Kayak
✉ Haulover Park, 10800 Collins Avenue ☎ 305/947 1302

Southern Florida and the Florida Keys

Everglades City
Everglades Rentals & Eco Adventures
✉ 107 Camilla Street
☎ 941/695 4666

Key West
Mosquito Coast Kayak Guides
✉ 1107 Duval Street
☎ 305/294 7178

Sanibel and Captiva Islands
Tarpon Bay
✉ 900 Tarpon Road (off Sanibel-Captiva Road near J N 'Ding' Darling Wildlife Refuge), Sanibel ☎ 941/472 8900

Central Florida

Ocala National Forest
Juniper Creek Canoe Run
✉ Juniper Springs Recreation Area, SR40 ☎ 352/625 2808

Northern Florida

Milton
Blackwater River State Park
Blackwater Canoe Rental
✉ 6974 Deaton Bridge Road, Milton ☎ 850/623 0235

Adventures Unlimited Outdoor Center
✉ Tomahawk Landing, SR87 (12 miles N of Milton)
☎ 850/623 6197

Cycling

Florida is as flat as a pancake and provides no challenges for the serious mountain biker, but it can be fun for a gentle spin. Bike rental is readily available in many resorts. There is a cycle trail around Palm Beach (➤ 21), the 47-mile Pinellas Trail in the Pinellas Suncoast area (➤ 63), and miles of cycle paths in quieter spots such as Sanibel and Captiva Islands (➤ 24). Two cycle trails in northern Florida are the 16-mile Tallahassee-St Marks Historic Railroad Trail which starts 4 miles south of Tallahassee on SR363; and the 17-mile Gainesville– Hawthorne State Trail, which crosses Payne's Prairie State Preserve.

Diving and Snorkelling

Coral reefs, wrecks, artificial reef sites and freshwater springs provide a terrific variety of diving and snorkelling experiences in destinations throughout the state. Anyone can snorkel off the beach or in Florida's pure freshwater springs, such as Blue Spring (► 53), and Wakulla Springs (► 89).

In the Florida Keys and the southeast a large number of dive operators offer instruction, equipment rental and trips for snorkellers and certified divers to North America's only living coral reef, which stretches for 220 miles just off the Atlantic coast. The Gold Coast resorts of Fort Lauderdale and Palm Beach also boast a number of man-made reef sites fashioned from scuppered ships, bridge spans and oil platforms (► 110, panel). The main Gulf coast dive centres are Panama City Beach and the Emerald Coast in Northern Florida. Below is a small selection of local operators.

Miami

Biscayne National Park Tours
✉ Convoy Point, 9700 SW 328th Street, Homestead
☎ 305/230 1100

South Beach Divers
✉ 850 Washington Avenue, Miami Beach ☎ 305/531 6110

Southern Florida and the Florida Keys

Fort Lauderdale
Pro Dive
✉ 515 Seabreeze Boulevard/A1A ☎ 954/761 3413

Islamorada
Bud n' Mary's Dive Center
✉ Mile Marker 79.8
☎ 305/664 2211

Key Largo
John Pennekamp Coral Reef State Park Dive Shop
✉ Mile Marker 102.5
☎ 305/451 6322

Lower Keys
Looe Key National Marine Sanctuary Dive Center
✉ Mile Marker 27.5, Ramrod Key ☎ 305/872 2215

West Palm Beach
Seapro Dive Center
✉ US1 at 37th Street, Riviera Beach ☎ 561/844 3483

Northern Florida

Destin
Scuba Tech
✉ Captain Dave's Marina, 312 US98 ☎ 850/837 2822

Panama City Beach
Hydrospace Dive Shop
✉ Hathaway Marina, 6422 W Highway 98 ☎ 850/234 3063

Fishing

Freshwater fishing on lakes and rivers and saltwater fishing from piers, bridges and off the beach itself is a way of life in Florida. Anglers over 16 may require state fishing licences, which can be bought at any of the bait-and-tackle shops.

The rich Gulf of Mexico fishing grounds, and the Gulf Stream off the Atlantic coast spell huge rewards for deep-sea sport fishermen. The Atlantic sailfish, marlin, tarpon, amberjack, bonito, grouper, snapper and pompano are among the prize catches pursued by charter fishing vessels from the Florida Keys to Fort Lauderdale, and from the Panhandle fishing centres of Destin and Fort Walton.

Ranger Programmes
A great way to get a real insight into local flora, fauna and history is to check out the ranger programmes offered by many state and national parks. Ranger-led bird-watching and nature walks reveal all sorts of interesting snippets of information, and you can be sure the ranger's practised eye will catch details that are easy to miss. During the winter high season, several parks host evening campfire programmes, which are a big hit with children.

Across the State by Boat

Strange but true, you can cruise around most of Florida without ever hitting the open sea. Florida's Intracoastal Waterway is one of the world's most travelled water highways. It runs down the Atlantic coast from Fernandina Beach to Miami, protected from the open sea by a chain of barrier islands. A 150-mile section cuts across the state from Stuart on the Atlantic to Fort Myers on the Gulf of Mexico, where the barrier islands pick up again and accompany the route most of the way round to Pensacola.

Golf

There are over 1,100 golf courses in the state, many of championship standard. Some of the finest are operated by resort hotels, and many Florida hotels offer good value golfing packages. The cooler winter months are the best; during summer it is advisable to play early in the day to avoid the worst of the heat and afternoon showers. Top destinations include the Gold Coast, Naples, Orlando and Walt Disney World, and Ponte Vedra Beach near Jacksonville. A complete guide to Florida's private and public courses *Fairways in the Sunshine* is available from:
Florida Sports Foundation 2930 Kerry Forest Parkway, Tallahassee, FL 32308-2000 ☎ 850/488 8347

Hiking

Florida has over 60 state and national parks and forests, which provide a wealth of unspoilt hiking territory. Most offer a choice of short, well-marked nature trails and longer-distance hiking paths. Beach preserves, such as the Canaveral National Seashore and the Gulf Islands National Seashore in the Panhandle, are also wonderful for walking. For overnight camping trips backcountry hiking permits must be obtained from ranger stations. Mosquitoes can be a problem even on short excursions, so be sure to carry a good repellent, and take plenty of water.

Tennis

There are more than 7,700 tennis facilities across the state. As well as municipal facilities and full-time tennis camps, many hotels have courts, and several major sporting resort hotels offer tennis packages with coaching. For a full listing, contact:
USTA (Florida Section) 1280 SW 36th Avenue, Pompano Beach, FL 33069 ☎ 954/968 3434

Watersports

Windsurfing, water-skiing, jet-skiing and dinghy sailing are all popular pastimes around Florida's coast. Hotel watersports clubs and beachfront concessions rent out equipment. Determined surfers can try their luck on the Atlantic coast, but the waves are pretty tame. Central Florida's lakes are also popular for water-skiing.

If you rent a motorboat or a jet-ski keep a sharp lookout for Manatee Zones and cut your speed where requested.

Dolphin Encounters

While this is not exactly a sport, swimming with dolphins is very popular. Several organisations in the Florida Keys offer dolphin encounters, but book well in advance:

Marathon
Dolphin Encounter ☎ 305/743 7000

Key Largo
Dolphins Plus ☎ 305/451 1993

Grassy Key
Dolphin Research Centre ☎ 305/289 1121

Islamorada
Theater of the Sea ☎ 305/664 2431

Spectator Sports

American Football

Florida has three National Football League (NFL) teams who are based in Miami, Jacksonville and Tampa.

Jacksonville Jaguars
✉ 1 Alltel Stadium Place
☎ 904/633 6050

Miami Dolphins
✉ Pro Player Stadium, 2269 Dan Marino Boulevard
☎ 954/452 7000

Tampa Bay Buccaneers
✉ 4201 N Dale Mabry Highway
☎ 813/879 BUCS

Baseball

The state's only major league baseball team is the Florida Marlins, based in Miami. However, spring training (Feb–Apr) brings other opportunities (► panel).

Florida Marlins
✉ Pro Player Stadium, 2269 Dan Marino Boulevard
☎ 305/626 7400

Basketball

Florida's most successful basketball team is based in Orlando, and there is another venue in Miami.

Miami Heat
✉ American Airlines Arena, 601 Biscayne Boulevard
☎ 786/777 4328

Orlando Magic
✉ 8701 Maitland Summit Boulevard ☎ 407/916 2643

Golf

Championship courses around the state host dozens of golfing events every year, including some PGA events. For information, contact:

PGA Tour
✉ 112 TPC Boulevard, Ponte Vedra Beach, FL 32082
☎ 904/285 3700

Motor Racing

The top local events are the Marlboro Grand Prix of Miami at Homestead-Miami Speedway (Feb) and the Daytona 500 and Speed Weeks (Feb).

Daytona International Speedway
✉ 1801 W International Speedway Boulevard
☎ 904/253 RACE

Homestead-Miami Speedway
✉ 1 Speedway Boulevard
☎ 305/230 7223

Polo

World-class and championship matches (Dec–Apr).

Palm Beach Polo, Golf and Country Club
✉ 11199 Polo Club Road, Wellington ☎ 561/798 7000

Royal Palm Polo Sport Club
✉ 18000 Jog Road, Boca Raton
☎ 561/994 1876

Tennis

Tennis has a huge following in Florida. Watch the world's top players compete in these major local tournaments:

Bausch & Lomb Women's Championships (Apr)
✉ Amelia Island Plantation
☎ 1-800 486 8366

Ericsson Open Tennis Championships (Mar)
✉ Tennis Center at Crandon Park, Key Biscayne (Miami)
☎ 305/442 3367

Spring Training

More than three-quarters of the nation's major league baseball teams muster in Florida for spring training. The highest concentration of visiting teams is found in the central Florida region, where cities such as Kissimmee, Clearwater and Tampa, as well as Walt Disney World itself, welcome the likes of the Houston Astros, Philadelphia Phillies and New York Yankees. Training games are played as part of the Grapefruit League, tickets are cheap, and the action is fast and furious.

Nightlife

Nightclubbing

There are nightclubs in all Florida's major cities, but the most dynamic and impressive scene is (not surprisingly) Miami Beach's SoBe district. A cover charge should not cost more than about $10, except for multi-venue complexes such as Orlando's Church Street Station and Walt Disney World's Pleasure Island (nearer $20). In line with Florida's drinking laws, most nightclubs will refuse entry to guests under 21, which is a major disappointment for many overseas visitors. It is advisable to carry a passport or some other proof of age.

Miami

Amnesia
One of the hottest dance spots on the beach. It is predominantly gay, but there are several mixed nights.
✉ 136 Collins Avenue, Miami Beach ☎ 305/531 5535
🕐 Nightly

Bash
Happening straight club with a sprinkling of celebrities, models and the like. There are dance floors indoors and out in a courtyard.
✉ 655 Washington Avenue, Miami Beach ☎ 305/538 2274
🕐 Nightly

Café Nostalgia
A taste of pre-Revolutionary hedonism, live Cuban music and lashings of nostalgia in Little Havana.
✉ 2212 SW 8th Street
☎ 305/541 2631 🕐 Thu–Sun 9PM–3AM

Clevelander
A bar and Ocean Drive landmark with exceptional people-watching potential. Every evening the pool area is packed
✉ 1020 Ocean Drive, Miami Beach ☎ 305/531 3485
🕐 Nightly until 5AM

Club Tropigala
Big-production, heavily besequinned musical revues to delight those who appreciate the full-on Las Vegas showtime approach.
✉ Fontainebleau Hilton, 4441 Collins Avenue, Miami Beach
☎ 305/672 7469 🕐 Nightly

Groove Jet
Hip SoBe dance club hideaway with an experimental edge to its musical offerings. House, trance and jungle are equally at home here.
✉ 323 23rd Street, Miami Beach ☎ 305/532 2002
🕐 Thu–Sun 11PM–5AM

The Improv
Miami's comedy showcase for the established and not-so-established.
✉ 3399 Virginia Street (Streets of Mayfair), Coconut Grove
☎ 305/441 8200 🕐 Tue–Sun

Jazid
This cool jazz venue in SoBe is just the place to simmer away on a tropical evening.
✉ 1342 Washington Avenue, Miami Beach ☎ 305/673 9372
🕐 Mon–Sat

Tobacco Road
Historic live blues venue in the heart of the downtown district, which also features regular jazz nights.
✉ 626 S Miami Avenue
☎ 305/374 1198 🕐 Nightly until 5AM

Van Dyke Café
Upstairs at the Van Dyke offers a great café-restaurant setting for some of the best jazz acts around plus blues and Latin American sounds.
✉ 846 Linclon Road, Miami Beach ☎ 305/534 3600
🕐 Nightly

Southern Florida and the Florida Keys

Fort Lauderdale
O'Hara's Pub
One of the top live jazz venues in the southeast. Also Sunday lunchtime sessions.
✉ 722 E Las Olas Boulevard
☎ 954/524 1764 🕐 Nightly

Islamorada
Woody's

Blue humour, live rock and roll and laser karaoke for a boisterous crowd.

✉ **Mile Marker 82** ☎ **305/664 4335** 🕐 **Daily, Mon until 2AM; Tue–Sun until 4AM**

Key West
Rick's

Popular nightspot with live music downstairs and dancing in the Upstairs Bar.

✉ **202 Duval Street** ☎ **305/296 5513** 🕐 **Café until 11pm; Bar 8pm–4am**

West Palm Beach
Respectable Street Café

Progressive nightclub in the downtown entertainment and dining district. Theme nights from techno and rave to retro.

✉ **518 Clematis Street** ☎ **561/832 0706** 🕐 **Tue–Sat from 9PM**

Central Florida

Kissimmee
Arabian Nights

Hugely popular dinner show featuring a glittering equestrian spectacular.

✉ **6225 W Irlo Bronson Memorial Highway/US192 (NM 8)** ☎ **407/239 9223 or 1-800 553 6116** 🕐 **Nightly**

Orlando
Church Street Station

One-time cover charge for admission to Phineas Phogg's high-energy discotheque; country music in the Cheyenne Saloon; rock and roll in the Orchid Garden; and Dixieland and more in Rosie O'Grady's Good Time Emporium.

✉ **129 W Church Street** ☎ **407/422 2434** 🕐 **Daily until 2AM**

Tampa
Green Iguana

A choice of bars, live bands, early evening jazz sessions at the heart of the Ybor City nightlife district.

✉ **1708 E 7th Avenue, Ybor City** ☎ **813/248 9555**

Walt Disney World
Downtown Disney Pleasure Island

A one-off admission fee covers entry to high-energy, 1970s retro and rock and roll discotheques, comedy and jazz clubs, plus an Old West-themed saloon bar.

✉ **Downtown Disney, E Buena Vista Drive** ☎ **407/934 7781** 🕐 **Nightly until 2AM**

Northern Florida

Daytona Beach
Razzle's

Dramatic light shows provide the namesake razzle to accompany chart and progressive sounds.

✉ **611 Seabreeze Boulevard** ☎ **904/257 6236** 🕐 **Daily 8PM–3AM**

Pensacola
Sluggo's

Three floors of bars, books, games, pool tables and live music at this distinctly wacky but hugely entertaining downtown venue.

✉ **130 Palafox Street** ☎ **850/435 0543** 🕐 **Tue–Sun 3PM–3AM**

Tallahassee
Dave's CC Club

North Florida's home of the blues also boasts the best Cajun bbq this side of the Mississippi.

✉ **Sam's Lane (off Bradfordville Road)** ☎ **850/894 0181** 🕐 **Tue–Sat**

Bars and Cafés

Florida is well supplied with watering holes, from TV-lined sports bars and pub-style micro-breweries to sidewalk cafés and poolside tiki bars (South Seas island theme and exotic cocktails). Most lure in the early evening crowd with cut-price drinks (usually two-for-the-price-of-one deals) during Happy Hour, which generally runs from 4PM–7PM, though this is a distinctly flexible arrangement. At night, many bars in cities and tourist areas metamorphose into live music venues with no cover charge.

What's On When

Theme Park Celebrations

Public holidays are a great excuse for central Florida's theme parks to break out the fireworks and party hats to celebrate in style. In spring, Universal Studios hosts a spectacular six-week Mardi Gras (Feb–Mar), and Walt Disney World Resort's Magic Kingdom holds an enormous Easter Sunday Parade. Fireworks and marching bands accompany the Independence Day celebrations, and the run-up to Halloween is another favourite, with special parties at SeaWorld and Church Street Station as well as Disney's Magic Kingdom and Universal Studios. A few weeks later all the parks go to town for Christmas and New Year.

January

Art Deco Weekend (mid-Jan): Miami's Art Deco district hosts a street festival featuring period music, classic automobiles and fashions.

February

Daytona Speed Weeks (first three weeks): motor racing extravaganza.
Silver Spurs Rodeo (last weekend): cowboy skills on show in Kissimmee.

March

Annual Sanibel Shell Fair (first week): sea shell displays and crafts in America's top shelling spot.
Carnaval Miami (second weekend): the nation's biggest Hispanic festival with top entertainers and parades.

April

Pompano Beach Seafood Festival (last weekend): seafood, live music, arts and crafts on the Gold Coast.

May

Florida Folk Festival: musicians gather at the Stephen Foster State Cultural Center in White Springs.
SunFest (first week): Florida's premier music, arts, and boating celebration in West Palm Beach.

June

Fiesta of Five Flags (early Jun): boat and street parades, sandcastle contest and more in Pensacola.

July

Suncoast Offshore Grand Prix (Jun–Jul): regatta races, fishing tournaments and entertainment culminating in the big race on Sarasota Bay.

Independence Day (Jul 4): celebrations throughout the state.

August

Venice Seafood Festival: seafood cooking competitions and boat exhibitions attract crowds to this seaside town just south of Sarasota.

September

Las Olas Art Fair (early Sep): art sales, music and food along Fort Lauderdale's main shopping street.
Anything That Floats River Raft Race: family fun on the St Johns River at Deland; west of Daytona Beach.

October

Fantasy Fest (last week): Key West's Wild Halloween carnival with a distinctly Caribbean twist.
Jacksonville Jazz Festival (Oct/Nov): free weekend festival featuring a host of big name stars.

November

Amelia Heritage Festival (Thanksgiving–New Year): Civil War re-enactments and tours of Fernandina Beach's historic district.
Annual Chrysanthemum Festival: spectacular floral displays at Cypress Gardens in central Florida.

December

Mickey's Very Merry Christmas Party: festive celebrations at the Magic Kingdom in the Walt Disney World Resort (► panel).
Orange Bowl Parade (Dec 31): floats, bands, clowns and music in a nationally televised parade from Biscayne Boulevard, Miami.

Practical Matters

*Pedestrian and road signs are
clear and self-explanatory*

BEFORE YOU GO

WHAT YOU NEED

● Required					
○ Suggested					
▲ Not required	UK	Germany	USA	Netherlands	Spain
Passport/National Identity Card (Valid for 6 months after entry)	●	●	▲	●	●
Visa Waiver Form	●	●	▲	●	●
Onward or Return Ticket	●	●	▲	●	●
Health Inoculations (tetanus)	○	○	○	○	○
Health Documentation (reciprocal agreement) (► 123, Health)	▲	▲	▲	▲	▲
Travel Insurance	●	●	▲	●	●
Driving Licence (national or International Driving Permit)	●	●	●	●	●
Car Insurance Certificate	○	○	●	○	○
Car Registration Document	●	●	●	●	●

WHEN TO GO

Central Florida/Orlando

| | High season |
| | Low season |

22°C	23°C	25°C	27°C	27°C	30°C	32°C	32°C	30°C	28°C	25°C	22°C
JAN	FEB	MAR	APR	MAY	JUN	JUL	AUG	SEP	OCT	NOV	DEC
☀	☁	☁	☀	🌦	☔	☔	☔	🌦	🌦	☀	☀

☀ Sun   ☁ Cloud   ☔ Wet   🌦 Sunshine and showers

TOURIST OFFICES

In the UK:
Visit Florida
Roebuck House
1 Palace Street
London SW1E 5BA
☎ 01737 644882
For a free brochure, recorded information
hotline (60p per minute) 09001 600555

In the US:
Visit Florida
661 E Jefferson Street
Suite 300
Tallahassee
FL 32301
☎ 850/488 5607
www.flausa.com

WHEN YOU ARE THERE

ARRIVING

Most visitors to Florida arrive at the international airport gateways of Miami and Orlando. Some direct scheduled flights also arrive at Tampa, and charter flights to Sanford (for Orlando), Daytona, Fort Myers and Fort Lauderdale are increasingly popular. US domestic airlines serve numerous local airports.

Miami International Airport	Journey times
Miles to Miami Beach	N/A
10 miles	30 minutes
	25 minutes

Orlando International Airport	Journey times
Miles to city centre	N/A
9¼ miles	45 minutes
	30 minutes

MONEY

An unlimited amount of American dollars can be imported or exported, but amounts of over £10,000 must be reported to US Customs. US travellers' cheques ('checks' in America) are accepted as cash in most places (not taxis) as are credit cards (Amex, Visa, Access, Mastercard, Diners). Dollar bills come in 1, 2, 5, 10, 20, 50 and 100 denominations. Note that all dollar bills are the same size and colour – all greenbacks. One dollar is made up of 100 cents. Coins are of 1 cent (penny), 5 cents (nickel), 10 cents (dime), 25 cents (quarter) and one dollar.

TIME

Local time in Florida is Eastern Standard Time (GMT –5), with the exception of the Pan-handle region, west of the Apalachicola River, which is on Central Standard Time (GMT –6). Daylight saving applies (Apr–Oct).

CUSTOMS

YES

There are duty-free allowances for non-US residents over 21 years of age:

Alcohol: spirits (over 22% volume):	1L
Wine:	1L
Cigarettes:	200 or
Cigars:	50 or
Tobacco:	2kg
Duty-free gifts:	$100

provided the stay in the US is at least 72 hours and that gift exemption has not been claimed in the previous six months. There are no currency limits.

NO

Meat or meat products, dairy products, fruits, seeds, drugs, lottery tickets or obscene publications. Never carry a bag through customs for anyone else.

CONSULATES

UK
☎ 305/374 1522
(Miami)

Germany
☎ 305/358 0290
(Miami)

Netherlands
☎ 305/789 6646
(Miami)

Spain
☎ 305/446 5511
(Miami)

WHEN YOU ARE THERE

TOURIST OFFICES

There are Local Visitor Information Offices at:
Fort Lauderdale:
● 1850 Eller Drive, Suite 303
  ☎ 954/765 4466

Fort Myers (Sanibel and Captiva Islands)
● 2180 W First Street, Suite 100
  ☎ 941/338 3500

Key West:
● 402 Wall Street
  ☎ 305/294 2587

Miami:
● 701 Brickell Avenue, Suite 2700
  ☎ 305/539 3000

Orlando:
● 8723 International Drive, Suite 101
  ☎ 407/363 5800

Palm Beach:
● 45 Coconut Row
  ☎ 561/655 3282

Pensacola:
● 1401 E Gregory Street
  ☎ 850/434 1234

St Augustine:
● 88 Riberia Street
  ☎ 904/829 1711

St Petersburg:
● 14450 46th Street N
  ☎ 727/464 7200

Sarasota:
● 655 N Tamiami Trail
  ☎ 941/957 1877

NATIONAL HOLIDAYS

J	F	M	A	M	J	J	A	S	O	N	D
2	1	(1)	(1)	1		1		1	2	2	2

1 Jan	New Year's Day
Jan (third Mon)	Martin Luther King Day
Feb (third Mon)	President's Day
Mar/Apr	Good Friday
May (last Mon)	Memorial Day
4 July	Independence Day
Sep (first Mon)	Labor Day
Oct (second Mon)	Columbus Day
11 Nov	Veterans' Day
Nov (fourth Thu)	Thanksgiving
25 Dec	Christmas Day

Boxing Day is not a public holiday in the US. Some shops open on National Holidays.

OPENING HOURS

○ Shops ● Post Offices
● Offices ◐ Museums/Monuments
● Banks ◐ Pharmacies

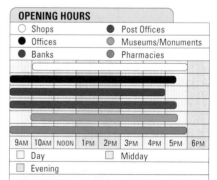

| 9AM | 10AM | NOON | 1PM | 2PM | 3PM | 4PM | 5PM | 6PM |

☐ Day ☐ Midday
▨ Evening

Shopping malls stay open until 9PM or later during the week, and many open on Sundays from around 11–5. Stores in resort areas may also keep more flexible hours. Post offices are not always easy to find and are closed on Saturdays; hotels will often help with basic postal needs. Theme park opening hours vary seasonally. Museum hours also vary; many close on Mondays, but stay open late one night a week. There are 24-hour pharmacies in all major towns; details will be posted at other pharmacies.

DRIVE ON THE
RIGHT

TOILETS
FREE

★ ★
★ ★

PUBLIC TRANSPORT

 Air US domestic carriers serve local airports in all Florida's major cities and holiday destinations. International airports such as Orlando receive direct flights from around 70 different US destinations. Domestic APEX airfares are very reasonable and it is well worth shopping around for good deals.

Trains Daily Amtrak (☎ 1-800/USA RAIL) services from Washington DC arrive the following day at Orlando (22 hours), Miami (27 hours), and Tampa (28 hours). The overnight AutoTrain service carries cars and passengers from Lorton, VA to Sanford (for Orlando). There is also a tri-weekly cross-country service from Los Angeles via the Panhandle for Miami. Train services within Florida are very limited; visitors to the southeast can use the inexpensive Tri-Rail commuter network which links Miami and West Palm Beach via Fort Lauderdale and Boca Raton.

Buses Greyhound buses provide a fairly comprehensive network of routes linking Florida's main cities and towns (☎ 1-800/ 231 2222). Passes for unlimited travel from four to 60 days are best purchased overseas, though savings are available on advance purchase tickets within the US. Local bus services are infrequent.

Urban Transport Door-to-door airport shuttle bus services to downtown and resort areas are a cheap and convenient alternative to taxis. Urban bus routes are generally geared towards commuters, although Orlando is well served by Lynx buses and the I-Ride service along International Drive. In Miami, some Metrobus services can be used for sightseeing; downtown is served by the elevated Metromover and the Metrorail light rail link; and there are Metrorail connections to Coconut Grove and Coral Gables.

CAR RENTAL

 The best way to get around in Florida. Rates are very competitive. Take an unlimited mileage deal, collision damage waiver and adequate (more than minimal) insurance. There is a surcharge on drivers under 25 and the minimum age is often 21 (sometimes 25).

TAXIS

 Taxis ('cabs'), can be picked up from the airport or hotel or booked by telephone (see Yellow Pages). Rates are around $2.50 for the first mile and around $1.50 for each additional mile. Water taxi services are available in Miami, Fort Lauderdale and Jacksonville.

DRIVING

 Speed limit on interstate highways: **55–65mph**

 Speed limit on main roads: **55–65mph**

 Speed limit on urban roads: **20–35mph**. All speed limits are strictly enforced.

 Seat belts must be worn by drivers and front seat passengers. Child seats are mandatory for under-threes; older children need a safety seat or seat belt.

 There are tough drinking and driving laws. Limit: 0.08 per cent of alcohol in blood. Opened cans or bottles containing alcohol in cars are illegal.

 Fuel (gasoline) is cheaper in America than in Europe. It is sold in American gallons (five American gallons equal 18 litres) and comes in three grades, all unleaded. Many gas stations have automatic pumps that accept notes and major credit cards.

 If you break down pull over, raise the bonnet (hood), turn on the hazard lights and call the rental company or the breakdown number (on or near the dashboard). The American Automobile Association (AAA) provides certain reciprocal facilities to affiliated motoring organisations in other countries. For AAA breakdown assistance ☎ 1-800/222 4357 (toll free).

PERSONAL SAFETY

Florida is not generally a dangerous place but to help prevent crime and accidents:

- Never open your hotel room door unless you know who is there. If in doubt call hotel security.
- Always lock your front and/or patio doors when sleeping in the room or going out. Use the safety chain/lock for security.
- When driving keep all car doors locked.
- If lost, stop in a well-lit gas station or ask for directions in a hotel, restaurant or shop.
- Never approach alligators, as they can outrun a man.

Police assistance:
☎ **091**
from any call box

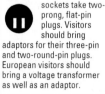

TELEPHONES

Making telephone calls from hotel rooms is expensive. Public telephones are found in hotel lobbies, drugstores, restaurants, gas stations and at the roadside. A local call costs 25 cents. Dial '0' for the operator. To 'call collect' means to reverse the charges.

International Dialling Codes	
From Florida (US) to:	
UK:	011 44
Ireland:	011 353
Australia:	011 61
Germany:	011 49
Netherlands:	011 31
Spain:	011 34

POST

Post offices in Florida are few and far between. Vending machines sell stamps at a 25 per cent premium; it is best to purchase them at their face value in your hotel. Post offices are usually open Mon–Fri 9–5; hotels and major attractions often provide postal services.

ELECTRICITY

The power supply is:
110/120 volts AC (60 cycles)

Type of socket:

sockets take two-prong, flat-pin plugs. Visitors should bring adaptors for their three-pin and two-round-pin plugs. European visitors should bring a voltage transformer as well as an adaptor.

TIPS/GRATUITIES

Yes ✓ No ✗		
It is useful to carry plenty of small notes		
Restaurants (if service not included)	✓	15–20%
Cafeterias/fast-food outlets	✗	
Bar Service	✓	15%
Taxis	✓	15%
Tour guides (discretionary)	✓	
Hotels (chambermaid/doorman etc)	✓	$1
Porters	✓	$1 per bag
Hairdressers	✓	15%
Toilets (rest rooms)	✗	

What to photograph: Florida's colourful theme parks are great places to take pictures. There are plenty of opportunities to take good beach snaps, and flora and fauna, too. Always protect cameras from sand and water.

When to photograph: avoid the glare of midday for the best results. Use a fast film (400ASA) for night-time shots.

Where to buy film: all types of film and photo processing are available in drug stores and theme parks.

HEALTH

Insurance
Medical insurance cover of at least $1,000,000 unlimited cover is strongly recommended, as medical bills can be astronomical and treatment may be withheld if you have no evidence of means to pay.

Dental Services
Your medical insurance cover should include dental treatment, which is readily available, but expensive. Have a check-up before you go. Dental referral telephone numbers are in the Yellow Pages telephone directory or ask at your hotel.

Sun Advice
By far the most common cause of ill health among visitors to Florida is too much sun. Use sunscreen on the beach and when sightseeing. Ensure that everyone drinks plenty of fluids. For minor sunburn, aloe vera gel is very soothing.

Drugs
Medicines can be bought at drugstores, though certain drugs generally available elsewhere require a prescription in the US. Acetaminophen is the US equivalent of paracetamol. Use an insect repellent containing DEET, and cover up after dark to avoid being bitten by mosquitoes.

Safe Water
Tap water is drinkable throughout Florida, though not particularly palatable. Mineral water is cheap and readily available. Restaurants usually provide customers with a jug of iced tap water.

CONCESSIONS

Students/Youths: Many sights and attractions offer special admission prices to students in possession of an International Student Identity Card. Children under three are generally allowed into attractions free; children's tickets are usually available up to age 12. Teenagers often have to pay the full adult rate.

Senior Citizens (Seniors): Florida offers special deals for senior citizens from discounted admission to museums and other sightseeing attractions to reduced room rates in hotels during the low season. Minimum age limits can vary, but many aged over 55 will qualify.

CLOTHING SIZES

Florida (USA)	UK	Rest of Europe	
36	36	46	
38	38	48	
40	40	50	
42	42	52	
44	44	54	
46	46	56	Suits
8	7	41	
8.5	7.5	42	
9.5	8.5	43	
10.5	9.5	44	
11.5	10.5	45	
12	11	46	Shoes
14.5	14.5	37	
15	15	38	
15.5	15.5	39/40	
16	16	41	
16.5	16.5	42	
17	17	43	Shirts
6	8	34	
8	10	36	
10	12	38	
12	14	40	
14	16	42	
16	18	44	Dresses
6	4.5	38	
6.5	5	38	
7	5.5	39	
7.5	6	39	
8	6.5	40	
8.5	7	41	Shoes

WHEN DEPARTING

- Allow plenty of time to reach the airport. Rental car depots are usually outside the airport and you will need to take a shuttle bus to the terminal.
- Check-in is at least two hours before departure time.
- Duty-free goods purchased at the airport are delivered to passengers at the door to the plane before take-off.

LANGUAGE

The official language of the US is English, and, given that one third of all overseas visitors come from the UK, Florida's natives have few problems coping with British accents and dialects. Hotel staff in larger tourist hotels may speak other European languages; Spanish is widely spoken, as many workers in the hotel and catering industries are of Latin American origin. However, many English words have different meanings in the US, below are some of the words most likely to cause confusion:

holiday	*vacation*	tap	*faucet*
fortnight	*two weeks*	rooms with	*efficiencies*
ground floor	*first floor*	cooking facilities	
first floor	*second floor*	luggage	*baggage*
flat	*apartment*	hotel porter	*bellhop*
holiday	*condominium,*	chambermaid	*room maid*
apartment	*condo*	surname	*last name*
lift	*elevator*	cupboard	*closet*

cheque	*check*	25 cent coin	*quarter*
travellers'	*travelers'*	banknote	*bill*
cheque	*check*	banknote	*greenback*
1 cent coin	*penny*	(colloquial)	
5 cent coin	*nickel*	dollar (colloquial)	*buck*
10 cent coin	*dime*	cashpoint	*automatic teller*

grilled	*broiled*	biscuit	*cookie*
frankfurter	*hot dog*	scone	*biscuit*
prawn	*shrimp*	sorbet	*sherbet*
aubergine	*eggplant*	jelly	*jello*
courgette	*zucchini*	jam	*jelly*
maize	*corn*	confectionery	*candy*
chips (potato)	*fries*	spirit	*liquor*
crisps (potato)	*chips*	soft drink	*soda*

car	*automobile*	petrol	*gas, gasoline*
bonnet (of car)	*hood*	railway	*railroad*
boot (of car)	*trunk*	tram	*streetcar*
repair	*fix*	underground	*subway*
caravan	*trailer*	platform	*track*
lorry	*truck*	buffer	*bumper*
motorway	*freeway*	single ticket	*one-way ticket*
main road	*highway*	return ticket	*round-trip ticket*

shop	*store*	nappy	*diaper*
chemist (shop)	*drugstore*	glasses	*eyeglasses*
bill (in a	*check*	policeman	*cop*
restaurant)		post	*mail*
cinema	*movie theatre*	postcode	*zip code*
pavement	*sidewalk*	ring up,	*call*
subway	*underpass*	telephone	
gangway	*aisle*	long-distance	*trunk call*
toilet	*rest room*	call	
trousers	*pants*	autumn	*fall*

Acknowledgements

The Automobile Association wishes to thank the following photographers, libraries and associations
for their assistance in the preparation of this book.
© 1998 BUSCH GARDENS TAMPA BAY, INC. All rights reserved. 64b; © DISNEY ENTERPRISES,
INC. 26b, 70, 71; MARY EVANS PICTURE LIBRARY 10b; HEMINGWAY HOUSE 14b; INTERNA-
TIONAL SPEEDWAY CORPORATION 74/5; KENNEDY SPACE CENTER, FLORIDA 8b; MRI
BANKER'S GUIDE TO FOREIGN CURRENCY 119; ORLANDO/ORANGE COUNTY CONVENTION
AND VISITORS BUREAU 53
The remaining photographs are held in the Association's own photo library (AA PHOTO LIBRARY), the
following were taken by: PETE BENNETT F/cover (d) Tallahasse clock, (g) sun
symbol, (h) catamaran sail, (i) lady sunbathing, (k) Art Deco building, 5b, 6a, 6b, 7a, 8a, 9a, 9b, 9c, 10a,
11a, 12a, 13a, 13b, 13c, 14a, 17b, 22b, 28b, 37b, 45b, 51, 52a, 52b, 54, 55a, 55b, 56a, 56/7, 57, 58a,
59a, 59b, 60, 61b, 62a, 62b, 63, 64a, 65a, 66, 67, 68a, 68b, 72, 76, 77a, 78b, 79b, 80b, 81a, 82b, 82c,
83a, 84b, 85a, 86b, 87b, 88, 89; JON DAVISON F/cover (b) sign post, 1, 20b, 27a, 28a, 29, 30, 31,
34a, 36, 37a; DAVID LYONS 7c, 16b, 33, 34b, 35; PAUL MURPHY B/cover Busch Gardens, 117b;
LANNY PROVO 5a, 38, 42b; TONY SOUTER F/cover (j) flamingo, bottom conch shells, 2, 6c, 11b, 39,
42a, 45a, 46, 47a, 58b, 61a, 61c, 73, 83b, 91b; the remainder were taken by JAMES A TIMS.

Emma Stanford wishes to thank Tanya Nigro at Florida Tourism in London and the many regional
tourist offices throughout Florida for their invaluable help.

Copy Editor: Penny Phenix   **Page Layout:** Barfoot Design
Revision Management: Outcrop Publishing Services, Cumbria

Dear Essential Traveller

Your comments, opinions and recommendations are very important to us. So please help us to improve our travel guides by taking a few minutes to complete this simple questionnaire.

You do not need a stamp (unless posted outside the UK). If you do not want to cut this page from your guide, then photocopy it or write your answers on a plain sheet of paper.

Send to: **The Editor, AA World Travel Guides, FREEPOST SCE 4598, Basingstoke RG21 4GY.**

Your recommendations…

We always encourage readers' recommendations for restaurants, nightlife or shopping – if your recommendation is used in the next edition of the guide, we will send you a **FREE AA *Essential* Guide** of your choice. Please state below the establishment name, location and your reasons for recommending it.

_____

_____

_____

_____

Please send me **AA *Essential*** _____
    (*see list of titles inside the front cover*)

About this guide…

Which title did you buy?
    AA *Essential* _____
Where did you buy it? _____
When? m m / y y

Why did you choose an AA *Essential* Guide? _____

_____

_____

_____

_____

Did this guide meet your expectations?
    Exceeded ☐ Met all ☐ Met most ☐ Fell below ☐
    Please give your reasons _____

_____

_____

_____

continued on next page…

Were there any aspects of this guide that you particularly liked? _____

_____

_____

_____

Is there anything we could have done better? _____

_____

_____

_____

_____

About you...

Name (*Mr/Mrs/Ms*) _____

   Address _____

_____

_____ Postcode _____

   Daytime tel nos _____

Which age group are you in?
   Under 25 ☐ 25–34 ☐ 35–44 ☐ 45–54 ☐ 55–64 ☐ 65+ ☐

How many trips do you make a year?
   Less than one ☐ One ☐ Two ☐ Three or more ☐

Are you an AA member? Yes ☐ No ☐

About your trip...

When did you book? m m / y y   When did you travel? m m / y y
How long did you stay? _____
Was it for business or leisure? _____
Did you buy any other travel guides for your trip?
   If yes, which ones? _____

_____

Thank you for taking the time to complete this questionnaire. Please send
it to us as soon as possible, and remember, you do not need a stamp
(*unless posted outside the UK*).

Happy Holidays!